DOING BUSINESS WITH ROMANIA

Donald E. deKieffer

Published by Business Books International, P O Box 1587, New Canaan, Connecticut 06840, U.S.A.

ISBN 0-916673-02-2

Typesetting and graphics: New Canaan Graphic Arts

AUTHOR

Donald deKieffer is a senior partner in the firm of Pillsbury, Madison & Sutro. From the firm's Washington office he advises and assists American and foreign clients on trade matters. Born in Newport, Rhode Island, in 1945, he received his law degree from Georgetown University. He served on the Senate Republican Policy Committee before entering private practice and completed a three-year stint as General Counsel to the U.S. Trade Representative before accepting his present position. He has been involved in extensive dealings with Romania in recent years.

INTRODUCTION

As a member of the Warsaw Pact, Romania at times exhibits an almost startling independence both in a political and economic sense. It is actively seeking to expand its business ties with the non-Communist world.

Although this guide provides the necessary historical, social and political backdrop necessary to understand Romania, we concern ourselves basically with economic and business issues.

It stands to reason that trading with and investing in Romania where government is the major entrepreneur, is hardly a matter of "business as usual" for businessmen from capitalistic societies.

Also, official red tape that is known to plague even the most enlightened of capitalistic societies, can become an insurmountable obstacle in Romania to those who do not prepare themselves properly.

The author not only briefs foreigners on the various official bodies that they are likely to encounter in striking deals with Romania. He also provides valuable advice on negotiating and pricing techniques, local business practices and customs, contracts and disputes, and all other issues of special importance to business.

As in our business guides on other countries, we attempted to produce a comprehensive but concise volume— complete, yet compact enough to accompany foreigners on their visit to Romania.

As in all other cases, the best business is obviously conducted on a first-hand basis. Some may find that apart from business, Romania also offers interesting sights and pleasures at a variety of mountain and beach resorts.

CONTENTS

Chapter 1

PROFILE OF ROMANIA

GEOGRAPHY AND CLIMATE

At 91,699 square miles (237,500 square km.) Romania's area is slightly smaller than Great Britain, ranking 12th in Europe.

Romania's boundaries total 1,959 miles (3,190.6 km.) of which 1,294 miles (2,153 km.) are fluvial or maritime. Its neighbors are the Soviet Union (with a frontier of 826 miles on the east and north); Hungary (275 miles to the west); Yugoslavia (399 miles to the southwest); Bulgaria (367 miles to the south); and the Black Sea (152 miles on the east).

Transylvania

Romania forms a complex geographical unit centered on the core of the Transylvanian Plateau, around which the peaks of the Carpathians and their associated subranges and structural platforms form a series of crescents. Beyond this zone, the extensive plains of the south and east of the country, their development intensified by the courses of the Danube and its tributaries, form another fertile zone bounded by the nation's frontiers and the waters of the Black Sea.

This geographic unity is formed from the diversity of relief and underlying rocks, a rich flow of water and an associated carpet of vegetation, many species of animals and shades of climate and a variety of mineral resources.

Forests

Forests, extending all over Romania's territory in the past, have been gradually replaced by farming lands. Today, about 25 percent of Romania's total area is forest of which deciduous trees (oak, beech, elm, ash, sycamore, lime, *etc.*) form approximately 71 percent. Resinous trees (29 percent of the lumbering reserves) include spruce, fir and pine. Above 4,000 feet in altitude, the land is covered with alpine meadows. For the past five years, Romania has been engaged in an extensive reforestation program. For each tree cut down in Romania today, the law requires three to be planted.

Romania's fauna is one of the most varied in Europe, consisting of both common and extremely rare species. The mountain areas shelter chamois, brown bear, carpathian stag, wolves, lynx, martins and other furry creatures. Bear, fox, wild boar, deer, partridge and quail are typical of the highlands and plains. The Danube Delta is inhabited by hundreds of species of birds both migratory and local. The water fauna is also differentiated according to altitude: the swift mountain streams are populated with trout, the hill rivers with barbel and in the plains, rivers and lakes are alive with carp, bream and pike. Sturgeons abound in the lower Danube waters and dolphins, herring, mackerel and mullet in the Black Sea.

Climate

Romania's geographic situation in the southeastern portion of Europe has endowed it with a climate that is transitional between the temperate regions and the harsher extremes of the continental interior. In the central and western portions of the nation, humid Atlantic characteristics prevail; in the southeast, the continental influence of the Russian plains make themselves felt and in the extreme southeast there are touches of milder sub-mediterranean influences. This overall pattern is substantially modified by the rugged relief patterns of the country and there are many climatic zones induced by a complex series of altitudinal changes.

The average annual temperature is 52° Fahrenheit (11° Centigrade) in the south and 45° F. (7° C.) in the north, although there is much variation according to altitude and related factors. Extreme temperatures range from 111° F. (44° C.) in the south to −36° F. (−38° C.) in the mountainous areas. The average annual rainfall amounts to 26 inches (660 millimeters), but this conceals very high rainfall in the Carpathians reaching about 55 inches (1400 millimeters) a year — and the low rainfall in the southeast — about 16 inches (400 millimeters) a year.

The most frequent winds are humid, blowing from the northwest although the strongest winds are often the drier ones coming from the northeast. A hot southwesterly wind, the *Austru,* blows over western Romania particularly in summer. In winter, cold, dense air masses encircle the eastern portions of the nation, with icy northeasterly winds known as the *Crivat* blowing from the western steppes while the oceanic air masses from the Azores, blowing over the west of the country, bring rain to soften the effect of the severe cold.

HISTORY

Recent archaelogical excavations have revealed traces of uninterrupted habitation in Romania since the paleolithic age. The great Indo-European migration in the third millenium B.C. brought significant changes in the ethnic composition of the current Carpathian-Danubian area. During the Bronze Age (second millenium B.C.), the Thracian people took shape in that region. In the first millenium B.C., the Dacians acquired a definite identity among the other Thracian tribes in the Balkan Peninsula and established, in the latter half of that millenium, an original civilization of their own.

In the first century B.C., an independent Dacian state ruled by Burebista (70-44 B.C.) spread from Bohemia (current-day Czechoslovakia) to the Black Sea including the Greek cities on the coast. The Dacian state, temporarily divided after Burebista's death, re-emerged during the reign of Decebalus (87-106 A.D.).

In 101-102 A.D. and 105-106, the Roman Empire waged two wars conquering Dacia. Most of the country became a Roman Province for 165 years. By adopting their language and culture, the native Dacians became Romanized, and a new Latin-speaking Daco-Roman people was formed. After the withdrawal of the Roman Empire (271 A.D.), the Daco-Romans stayed on; they engaged in farming and herding and survived the invasions of the Nomadic people (Goths, Huns, *et.al.*) in the 6th through 12th centuries. Christianity began to spread in the 3rd century, and after the great schism of 1054, the Romanians remained in the fold of the Eastern Orthodox Church.

Written sources mention the emergence of the earliest Romanian feudal states in Transylvania (10th Century), Dobruja (11th Century), and east and south of the Carpathians (12-13th Centuries). In the 11-13th Centuries, the Hungarians, who had settled in Pannonia by the end of the 9th Century vanquished Transylvanian territory. These areas were eventually incorporated into the Hungarian Kingdom. Until 1541, however, Transylvania enjoyed a significant level of autonomy under Hungarian rule. The Romanian feudal domains east and south of the Carpathians formed the independent states of Wallachia and Moldavia. An independent feudal state which later united with Wallachia was also established in Dobruja, the region between the Danube and the Black Sea, in the first half of the 14th Century.

Middle Ages

Although the Romanians lived in three separate states (Wallachia, Moldavia and Transylvania) during the Middle Ages, their economic, political and cultural links were preserved and they retained a definitive national identity. By the end of the 14th Century, the Ottoman Empire extended as far as the Danube. The three Romanian lands embarked upon a period of national survival in which several personalities distinguished themselves. Mircea Cel Batrin (Mircea the old, 1386-1418), Stefan Cel Mare (Stephen the Great, 1457-1504), Iancu De Hunedoara (John Hunyadi, 1441-1453).

In the 16th Century, Wallachia and Moldavia were forced to recognize the Ottoman Suzerainty, while keeping a high degree of internal autonomy; in 1541, Transylvania became an autonomous principality of the Ottoman Empire. By the end of the 16th Century, Mihai Viteazul (Michael the Brave), Prince of Wallachia (1593-1601), began an anti-Ottoman war and united all three Romanian lands under his rule. Because of the opposition shown by the neighboring great powers (the Ottoman Empire, Austria and Poland) to the establishment of a strong Romanian state, it was shortlived, but it acquired a symbolic value in the subsequent centuries.

In the 17th Century the Romanian lands flourished under the rule of Matei Basarab (1632-1654), Vasile Lupu (1634-1653), George Racoczi I (1630-1648), and Constantin Brancoveanu (1688-1714). Taking advantage of the weakened position of the Ottoman Empire, Austria annexed the principality of Transylvania following the Peace of Karlowitz (1699). In the 18th and 19th centuries, the wars between Russia, Austria and Turkey were often waged in the region.

Austria temporarily annexed Oltenia (1718-1739) and Bucovina (1775-1918). After the Russian-Turkish War of 1806-1812, Bessarabia (the part of Moldavia between the Pruth and the Dniester) was incorporated by Russia (1812-1918). The revolution led by Tudor Vladimirescu in 1821 and the Bourgeois-Democratic Revolution of 1848-1849 in the three Romanian lands opened the way to their modern development and gave a strong impetus to the national liberation struggle.

Both revolutions were suppressed by the armed intervention of the Russian and Ottoman Empires. Wallachia and Moldavia remained under the suzerainty of the Ottoman Empire, and Transylvania under Austrian domination. In 1859, Wallachia united with Moldavia following the election of one ruling prince, Alexandru Ioan Cuza, in the two principalities.

Romania

In 1862 the new national state was officially named Romania. The Constitution enacted in 1866 declared Romania a constitutional monarchy; Carol of Hohenzollern-Sigmaringen became prince and then (in 1881) King of Romania. On May 9, 1877, Romania proclaimed its independence and participated on the Russian side in the war against Turkey (1877-1878). The Peace of San Stefano and the Treaty of Berlin (1878) recognized Romania's independence and restored its authority over

Dobruja. The union of the Romanian principalities and the winning of independence further stimulated the modern economic, social and political development of the country.

World War I

The last phase of the process leading to the establishment of the Romanian Unitary National State took place in the years of World War I. Romania maintained its neutrality for two years, then joined the Entente, in August, 1916, aiming to recover its national territories, which until then had been under foreign domination. The people of Bessarabia (on 9 April 1918), Bukovina (on 27 November 1918) and Transylvania (on 1 December 1918) opted for unification with Romania, thus completing the establishment of the Romanian Unitary National State. The union of 1918 favored industrial development and the establishment of modern political institutions.

World War II

At the outbreak of World War II, Romania declared its neutrality. On June 26, 1940, Bessarabia and northern Bucovina were incorporated by the USSR; on 7 September 1940 the southern port of Dobruja was incorporated by Bulgaria; and on August 30, 1940, the Vienna dictate ceded the northern part of Transylvania to Hungary.

During this period, Romania's government was dominated by the upper bourgeoise and remainder of the old land-owning aristocracy, based only nominally upon a liberal constitutional system with *de facto* limitation of sufferage. The Social Democratic Party which controlled the small labor movement, was tolerated by the monarchy but never had political power. The Romanian Communist Party was an underground movement at the time. In the 1930's an anti-Semitic, anti-Soviet fascist Iron Guard movement threatened the government which was taken over in 1940-1941 by the authoritarian general Antonescu.

In June 1941 Romania entered World War II on the side of the Axis powers. A coup led by King Michael and opposition politicians led by the Communist Party of Romania with the support of the army, deposed the Antonescu dictatorship on August 23, 1944 (Romania's national holiday). The next day, Romanian forces switched sides, entering the war against the Germans in Transylvania, Hungary and Czechoslovakia. Romania, which had suffered extensive losses in the war against the USSR, incurred additional heavy casualties.

Peace Treaty

The peace treaty signed at Paris on February 10, 1947, confirmed the Soviet annexation of Bessarabia and northern Bukovina and a largely Bulgarian-populated area of southern Dobrudja to Bulgaria. It also incorporated into Romania that portion of northern Transylvania granted to Hungary in 1940 under the Vienna dictate. In addition, the treaty required substantial war reparations by Romania to the Soviet Union and other allied states.

Soviet occupation forces supported communist organizers in Romania and the non-communist political leaders were purged. On March 6, 1945 King Michael was forced to appoint a communist-dominated government headed by Dr. Petry Groza, president of the Ploughman's Front. A number of so-called "historical parties" also participated in this government, led by Gh. Tatarescu, who assumed the office of vice-president of the Council of Ministers and Minister of Foreign Affairs (Tatarescu had been prime minister twice before, prior to 23 August 1944).

Peoples Republic

The King abdicated under pressure on December 30, 1947 and the Romanian Peoples Republic was declared.

Since late 1961, however, Romanian communism has assumed an increasingly nationalistic cast. A substantial shift in Romanian foreign policy has resulted. In 1965, the Romanian Peoples Republic was reconstituted as the Socialist Republic of Romania and in 1968, a sweeping reorganization of the administrative structure and territorial division was carried out. The new territorial division is reminiscent of that existing before the imposition of the Soviet-style regime.

POPULATION

As of December 31, 1981, Romania had a population of 22,400,000, ranking 8th in Europe and 33rd in the world. Romania's population is about the same as that of Canada.

ROMANIAN DEMOGRAPHICS

(1981)

Urban population:	46.90%
Birth rate:	1.80%
Death rate:	1.04%
Natural growth:	.76%
Average life expectancy:	69.82 years
Males:	67.42
Females:	72.18

Due to its high growth rate, Romania is a relatively "young" country compared with the developed nations of the world. Population structure by age is indicated in Chart 2.

POPULATION BY AGE

(1980)

0 to 4 years:	9.0%
5 to 14 years:	17.6%
15 to 24 years:	14.4%
25 to 34 years:	14.7%
35 to 44 years:	12.6%
45 to 54 years:	13.0%
55 to 64 years:	8.4%
65 to 74 years:	7.1%
over 75:	3.2%

In addition to its rather low average age, Romania is a remarkably homogeneous country, even by European standards.

POPULATION BY NATIONALITY

(1977)

Romanian:	88.14%
Magyar (Hungarian):	7.91%
German:	1.62%
Ukranian:	.25%
Serbian:	16%
Jewish:	.12%
Tartar:	.11%
Russian:	0.10%
Bulgarian:	0.05%
Other:	0.04%

Like many other newly industrialized countries, Romania has seen an explosive growth in urban population. In 1980, 46.9 percent of the total population was urban as opposed to 21.4 percent in 1930. It is estimated the urban population will grow to 55 percent by 1985 and to 65 percent by 1990.

Lineage

The Romanian people trace their lineage to Roman times and are related to French, Italians, Spanish and other "Latins." As a result, the Romanian language, although containing many elements of Slavic, Turkish and other languages, is related to French, Italian, Portuguese and Spanish.

Aside from the Romanians, most of the minority populations reside in Transylvania. Before World War II minorities represented more than 26 percent of the total population, but that percentage was halved in large part by the loss of the border areas of Bessarabia and northern Bukovina (to the USSR) and southern Dobruja (to Bulgaria), as well as by the postwar Diaspora of ethnic Germans. However, in Transylvania, which was a part of the pre-1918 Austria-Hungary, Romania retains areas where the ethnic minority sometimes makes up a substantial portion of the local population.

The official Romanian government policy toward national minorities is non-discriminatory and permits cultural autonomy; but it insists upon their integration into the national economy and provides for compulsory study of Romanian in addition to the minority languages. The Jewish community surviving World War II has been reduced about 90 percent over the past three decades by emigration to Israel. In recent years up to 10,000 of the nearly 400,000 ethnic Germans have emigrated annually to the Federal Republic of Germany. Since World War II, however, there has been little emigration of ethnic Hungarians to Hungary.

Language

The official language of Romania is Romanian, a Romance Language. It evolved directly from the Latin spoken in the Carpathian-Danubian-Balkan area. In addition to their native language, most Romanians speak at least one and often three or more foreign languages. The most common foreign languages are French, English, Russian and German.

Religion

Religious observance in Romania has traditionally been extensive and religious allegiances generally follow ethnic lines, with about 80 percent of all Romanians nominally belonging to the Romanian Orthodox Church. The Greek Catholic or Uniate Church to which about 10 percent of the populace belong, was incorporated into the Romanian Orthodox Church by fiat in 1948. Roman Catholics, largely Magyar and German, constitute about 6 percent of the population; Calvinists, Jews, Baptists and Lutherans make up most of the remaining 4 percent.

GOVERNMENT AND LEGAL SYSTEM

According to the constitution adopted in 1965, Romania is a state governed by, "... A socialist, sovereign independent and unitary state of the working people of the towns and villages." The constitution states that in the Republic, "... The leading political force of the whole society is the Romanian Communist Party."

Constitution

The 1965 constitution spells out the basic rights and duties of the citizens, the electoral system, the bodies of state power and administration, the local bodies of power and administration, the judicial bodies, and the prosecutors' offices.

It further provides for non-Romanian nationalities, "... [T]he free utilization of their native language as well as books, papers, magazines, theaters, and education at all levels in their own language." In districts where non-Romanian nationalities are living, "... All the bodies and institutions use the language of the respective nationality in speaking and in writing." "Anybody is free to share or not to share a religious belief but ... the school is separated from the church."

Guarantees

According to the Romanian constitution, the state guarantees equal rights for all citizens, regardless of nationality, race, sex or religion. It provides the right to work, to rest, to old age, to sickness or disability insurance, to education, to the free use of the mother tongue, to association, *etc.*

The 1965 Constitution guarantees Romanian citizens the freedom of expression, press, assembly, opinion, the inviolability of the home, person, correspondence, and telephone conversation. Their rights to petition, private personal property, and inheritance are also provided for in the constitution. Unlike the United States, however, it is the administration — not the courts — which ultimately determine the constitutionality of their actions.

The Constitution also provides for "citizens' duties" which include the observance of the law, safeguarding socialist property, strengthening and development of the socialist system, participation in national defense, and compulsory military service.

Government

The following organizations, bodies and individuals govern Romania:

Romanian Communist Party (RCP)

According to the constitution, the RCP is the leading political force in Romania. It is "... The highest form of organization of the working class, its vanguard detachment"; it "... Serves the vital interests and hopes of the people"; it bases its activities "... On the Marxist-Leninist teachings, applying it creatively to the specific conditions and particularities of Romania."

The RCP was founded on May 8, 1921; in 1948 it merged with the Social Democratic Party to form the Romanian Workers Party. It resumed its original name in 1965. In 1983, the RCP had 3,262,-000 members (21 percent of the adult population). The principal organs of the party are the Congress (the Supreme Body convened every five years), the Central Committee (in charge of all activities between the Congresses), the Executive Political Committee of the Central Committee (which manages the party activities between the plenary meetings of the Central Committee), and the Secretariat of the Central Committee (which verifies the implementation of decisions and carries out the personnel policies). The Secretary-General of the RCP is Nicolae Ceausescu.

Between Congresses, the Central Committee usually convenes a National Conference of the Party. Five such National Conferences have taken place so far (October 1945, December 1967, July 1972 and December 1977, December 1982).

The Central Committee, "... Guides the entire activity of the Party in the interval between Congresses"; it elects the Executive Political Committee of the Central Committee and the Secretariat. "Leadership of Party activity is insured between plenary meetings by the Politburo," states Article XXIV of the New Rules. The latter is the real policymaking body in Romania.

Socialist Democracy and Unity Front (SDUF)

This body was founded in 1980 and is the "grassroots" political body of the country. Organized under the Communist Party, all organizations are coordinated through it. The supreme body of the SDUF is the Congress, convened every five years. Between Congresses activities are managed by the National Council; between the plenary sessions of the Council by an Executive Bureau. The SDUF has its own branches, organized according to territorial and place-of-work principles, on a local and central level. The President of the SDUF is Nicolae Ceausescu.

Grand National Assembly (GNA)

The Assembly is the titular legislative authority of state power in the country. Following the elections of 9 March 1980, it has 369 deputies elected for a five-year term. The Assembly elects from its membership for one term the Bureau, six secretaries and eight permanent commissions, the Romanian group of the Interparliamentary Union and the Romanian parliamentary group for Security and Cooperation in Europe. The legislature performs its work in plenary sessions and in commissions.

Council of State

The bulk of legislative work is performed by the Council of State, a permanent body of 28 members elected by the GNA, which acts when the Assembly is not in session. The Council consists of a president, three vice-presidents, 23 members, and a secretary. Its president is the President of the Republic, Nicolae Ceausescu, who was elected to this position as the country's first president in March, 1974. The Council of State has the power to issue decrees with force of law.

President

In March 1974, the GNA created the office of the President of the Republic. The President is elected by the GNA for one term and is responsible to the Assembly. The President is the head of state and represents state power in the internal and international relations of Romania; he is also the President of the State Council, Commander-in-Chief of the Armed Forces, and Chairman of the Defense Council.

Council of Ministers

This is the "supreme body of state administration" charged with the overall management of state activities. According to the constitution, the government is elected by the Grand National Assembly for one term.

In fact, however, it executes the policies established by party leadership. The Council is composed of the Prime Minister (head of government), Prime Vicle-Premiers, Vice-Premiers, and Ministers and heads of various other central administrative organs.

Iron Gates hydropower plant

The Constitution gives the Council of Ministers extensive powers to carry out the state economic plan, manage the country's economy, insure public order, defend the interests of the state, protect the rights of citizens, direct the country's armed forces and military conscription, conduct foreign affairs, and suspend decisions of the County People's Councils which do not conform to the law. In fulfilling its functions, the Council of Ministers is authorized to issue decisions and orders. In March 1969, a Defense Council was formerly set up to take over many of the perogatives of the Council of Ministers with regard to defense matters.

Party/State Organizations

Following the July 1972 National Party Conference, several combined party and state bodies were formed to control a wide variety of party and government activities, further eroding the authority of the Council of Ministers. The Supreme Council for Economic and Social Development (SCESD), headed by President Ceausescu, was established in 1973 to coordinate all social and economic planning. Other new party and state organizations are the Council for Social and Economic Organizations, which controls the size and function of ministeries and economic enterprises, and the Central Council of Workers Control over Economic and Social Activities which oversees fulfillment of economic planned targets.

Legal System

The judiciary is constitutionally limited to, "... defending the socialist order and personal rights, educating citizens to the respect of the law," and by applying sanctions, "reeducating law breakers and preventing the commission of new infractions." A new revision of the judicial system is being designed to remove misdemeanors from the court system, reduce punishments for felonies, reduce the number of crimes punishable by death from 28 to 5 (exempting altogether youth and some women) and create workers' judicial councils to handle 40-50 percent of cases previously requiring court appearance.

None of the courts — the Supreme Court, the County Court, the People's Courts, *etc.* — has the authority to review the constitutionality of laws.

The Supreme Court guarantees uniformity of procedures by supervision and decision in procedural matters. It is elected anew by each GNA and is responsible to it or (between GNA sessions) to the Council of State. Theoretically, judges and assessors (lay judges) are independent and subject only to the law.

Chief Public Prosecutor

The office of the Chief Public Prosecutor has constitutional status. The Chief Public Prosecutor is vested with the, "... supreme supervisory power to insure the observance of the law by ministeries and other central organs, by the local organs of state power and administration, as well as by officials and other citizens."

The Arbitration Board

A State Arbitration Board oversees settlement of disputes concerning property between socialist economic units and between socialist organizations. These disputes can involve a wide range of questions including labor relations, contractual issues, jurisdictional disputes between governmental and parastatal institutions, *etc.*

POLITICS

The transition immediately after World War II from the pro-German dictatorship of Ion Antonescu to communist rule was swift. After proclaiming a Peoples Republic (30 December 1947), private enterprises were nationalized (on June 11, 1948), agricultural collectivization was initiated, industrial development speeded up and a Soviet-style centrally planned economy was adopted across the board.

However, a general "derussification" of the country began in 1961 as the Romanian leadership displayed an increasing independence of the Soviet Union whose troops were withdrawn in 1958. During the 1960's, the growth of political nationalism increasinglyasserted itself in both domestic and foreign policy.

By 1977, virtually all political prisoners had been released, and restrictions on a wide range of political and social activities were reduced or rescinded. Economic, political and cultural relations were expanded, not only with "socialist" countries but with the Western democracies and a number of less developed countries.

Acceptance

The Romanian government's nationalistic policies have won considerable popular acceptance. Increasing numbers of persons from those strata previously most antagonistic to the system — intellectuals and agricultural workers — joined the Romanian Communist Party. The party's membership rose from 1.3 million in 1965 to over 3.2 million or more than 10 percent of the total population by 1983.

Political leadership since the late 1950's has been remarkably stable, and the passage of power from long-time party/government chief Gheorghe Gheorghiu-Dej, who died in 1965 to Nicolae Ceausescu was smooth and uncomplicated. Ceausescu's two decades in office have been characterized by a gradually improving living standard and popular acceptance of the government's independent foreign policy.

Official visits

As if to underscore Romania's aggressively independent foreign policy, President Ceausescu makes frequent official visits abroad, and has become one of the best-known leaders in the Eastern bloc. He has also focused his attention on the third world. Hardly a week passes that he is not entertaining — or being entertained by — the president of some developing country.

There has been no evidence of any prospective change in Romania's policy of independence within the Communist system or its efforts to improve relations with non-communist governments. Responsible officials have repeatedly declared these policies will be continued.

FOREIGN RELATIONS

In 1983 Romania had diplomatic and consular relations with 137 states, economic relations with 150 and cultural relations with 120 countries.

Romania maintains by East European standards an independent foreign policy. It is an active member of the Group of 77 and has often taken positions at odds with those of other Council for Mutual Economic Assistance members.

Although it is not "non-aligned" (in view of its Warsaw Pact membership), Romania's almost startling independence in the area of foreign relations has given it a credibility with third world countries not enjoyed by any other Warsaw Pact member.

In particular, relationships in the Middle East are unique in the world. It not only maintains close diplomatic, economic and cultural ties with most of the Arab countries but is also the only Communist country which has good relations with Israel. In fact, Bucharest is the only destination in Eastern Europe for El Al, the Israeli state airline.

Middle East

Because of its carefully-cultivated independence, Romania has significant trade with both Arab countries and Israel. Significantly, Romania has never had a problem dealing with the Arab boycott and is a major center for entrepot trade between Western Europe and the Middle East.

Some American entrepreneurs have explored the possibility of using Romania as a base to conduct business in the Middle East given the favorable relationship that country cultivates with the Arabs. This possibility has already proven successful for European companies using Romania as go-between.

Romania foreign policy is also responsive to pragmatic business concerns in the Middle East. Romania rarely takes a position likely to jeopardize trade ties with any of the major parties in that part of the world as it has significant projects in countries as disparate as Iraq, Libya, Israel, Algeria and India.

In contrast to the Romanian authorities' lukewarm attitude with regard to penetrating the East European market using their country as a base of operations, they actively encourage Western entrepreneurs to cooperate with Romanian enterprises in Middle East markets.

Despite their lack of sophistication in marketing in the West, Romanians have proven skillful in many Middle East markets and there are literally thousands of Romanian engineers and sales representatives fluent in Arabic, located in Middle Eastern countries. Further, the Romanian government has made a low-key approach in the Middle East, striving not to offend any sensibilities.

Third World

This subdued approach is also evident in Romania's relationships with many of the emerging "third world" countries. Here, Romanian cooperation is almost exclusively economic as opposed to the military assistance programs touted by many other countries.

Romanians openly encourage on both an official and an unofficial level Western private enterprise to join them in either export or investment projects in third world countries. Some Western companies have found it politically desirable to enter third world markets under the aegis of Romania.

Before entering such arrangements in cooperation with Romania, however, especially American businessmen should seek legal advice concerning the applicability of American laws to their activities in any third country. As the Soviet pipeline dispute indicated, the mere fact that a company is registered in a foreign country may not necessarily insulate it from reach of U.S. law. Nevertheless, Romanian laws on the subject (particularly the fact that wholly-owned foreign subsidiaries are not permitted), might well protect U.S. joint venture or coproduction agreements with Romanian principals. (See FOREIGN INVESTMENT)

Romania already is engaged in extensive projects with 19 developing countries and is rapidly expanding its contacts in Africa and even South America.

As the expansion of Romanian enterprise in third world countries is a political as well as economic goal of the Romanian authorities, American entrepreneurs seeking Romanian cooperation in these areas should not neglect contacts in the Ministry of Foreign Trade.

CMEA

Romania pursues a very active foreign policy, responding to its specific interests. It is a member of the Council for Mutual Economic Assistance (CMEA), also referred to as COMECON, and the Warsaw Pact.

As a European country, it has taken an active part in security discussions with the rest of Europe and advanced proposals for making the Balkans a nuclear-free zone. It has also taken a leading position as a so-called "developing country" and is a member of a Group 77.

Where there's flavor, there's Felton.

We started out half a century ago to create the highest quality tobacco flavors. And we've never stopped trying to improve. Is it any wonder Felton tobacco flavors are used the world over today?

Felton INTERNATIONAL, INC. A WORLD LEADER IN CREATIVE FLAVORS AND INNOVATIVE TECHNOLOGY.

FELTON INTERNATIONAL, INC., 599 JOHNSON AVE., BKLYN, NY 11237, (212) 497-4664

AUSTRALIA CANADA FRANCE HONG KONG INDONESIA ITALY JAPAN MEXICO SPAIN UNITED KINGDOM

Over the past decade, however, the Romanian government has embarked upon a policy designed to avoid dependence upon any particular trading partner or bloc. Romania maintains important trade relations with the People's Republic of China and Yugoslavia. In recent years Romania's foreign trade with non-CMEA members has, for example, increased much faster than intra-CMEA trade. This trend shows every sign of continuing.

Despite this relative independence within the Eastern bloc in matters of commerce, finance and foreign policy, Romania maintains close relations with the other "Socialist" countries.

An important factor in Romania's foreign trade policy is that its currency is more freely convertible with other CMEA members than with most Western countries. Given the fact that none of the CMEA members' currencies are regarded as "hard" by the international monetary community, however, this does not necessarily augur well for an entrepreneur seeking to use Romania as a base for penetrating other Eastern European markets.

At the present time, Romania needs convertible currency. The main task of Romanian foreign trade policy is to insure a convertible foreign exchange surplus to finance the servicing of the country's external debt.

Exports to other Socialist states for equally soft currencies is not currently a high priority. Nevertheless, particularly in some consumer goods and heavy industrial areas, Romania is willing to assist Western businesses in penetrating Eastern European markets, particularly if the development of an industry in Romania has the effect of reducing imports.

Warsaw Pact

Romania is a charter member of the Warsaw Pact, the East European equivalent of NATO. Romania's defense expenditures are low by European standards. It has no significant armaments industry. Romania's independent foreign policy which emphasizes detente enables it to devote most of its resources to industrial and economic development instead of spending large amounts on armaments.

As a matter of politics and practicality, it is unlikely that Romania will be a significant factor in international arms trade in the foreseeable future either as a buyer or seller. One often gets the impression in Romania that on a private level, at least, Romanians regard the necessity for a large standing army with a great deal of distaste as it may deprive other potentially more productive sectors of necessary capital.

U.S. Relations

The United States and Romania have taken a number of actions in the past decade to support increased U.S.-Romanian commercial activity, including extension of Commodity Credit Corporation (CCC), U.S. Export-Import Bank, and Overseas Private Investment Corporation (OPIC) facilities.

Over a decade ago, the governments of both countries created the joint American-Romanian Economic Commission (AREC) to review the progress of bilateral economic and commercial problems and to discuss and resolve trade problems. The Commission meets annually. It is headed by the U.S. Secretary of Commerce and the Romanian Minister of Foreign Trade and International Economic Cooperation. In connection with Commission activities, trade officials from both countries often meet at the working level in numerous expert and working group meetings held on a regular basis.

Chapter 2

ECONOMIC SCENE

ECONOMY

After World War II, nationalization of commercial enterprises in Romania was followed by planned expansion. Between 1948 and 1955 more than 100 new industrial undertakings were built and 200 more were rebuilt and expanded.

Between 1948 and 1960 industrial production increased at an average annual rate of more than 16%. Overall it increased fivefold between 1938 and 1960.

Capital Goods

In the course of this industrial growth the balance was tipped away from consumer goods, which in 1938 made up for more than half of production, to capital goods which in the 1960's accounted for more than three-fifths.

Once a predominantly agrarian country, Romania has experienced high industrial growth since the 1950's. Since 1970 industrial production has risen at an average annual rate of more than 12% despite numerous natural disasters including a devastating earthquake in 1977.

Industry accounted for 50% of the country's national income in 1976 and has remained at approximately this level. The bigger growth has been experienced in the electronics, machine building, chemical, and metallurgical sectors. This was achieved at the expense of agricultural development and the Romanian consumer.

GNP

According to Western estimates the Romanian gross national product (GNP) reached $52.5 billion by 1977. Romanian per capita GNP was approximately $2,442, roughly four-fifths of that of most other East European countries.

About two-thirds of Romania's total investment goes to industry. More than 60% of industrial investment was devoted to electric power, metallurgy, machine building and chemical sectors. In recent years, energy and light industry have also been given priority.

Statistics

Romania, as is the case with many other East European countries, maintains statistics on an indexed rather than actual "hard number" basis. Nevertheless, the charts in the following pages serve as a general idea of economic progress in various areas.

It should be kept in mind, however, that the relative value of the lei changed during the period covered by these charts.

Even with these caveats, it is still apparent that the growth rates in almost every sector of the Romanian economy have been impressive whether calculated in constant dollar terms or on any other basis.

Since Romania is a state-controlled economy, taxes appear disproportionately low by Western standards. Further, such expenditures as national defense also appear low as a proportion of the state budget. It should be recognized, however, that such expenditures and income should be compared to gross national product rather than as a percentage of state expenditures.

INDEX OF ROMANIAN ECONOMIC DEVELOPMENT

(1965 = 100)

	1975	1980	1981	Average annual rate of growth 1966-1981 Percentage
Fixed Assets	239	371	402	9.1
Volume of Investments	293	441	410	9.2
Social Product	251	351	354	8.2
National Income	247	351	358	8.3
Gross Industrial Output	322	507	520	10.9
Group A (producer goods)	349	566	580	11.6
Group B (consumer goods)	269	390	401	9.1
Building & Assembly Output	233	309	294	7.0
Gross Agricultural Production	150	181	180	3.7
Retail Sales by Socialist Trade	215	314	325	7.6
Volume of Foreign Trade	406	841	851	14.3
Per capita National Income	221	300	305	7.2
State Budget Expenditure on Socio-Cultural Actions	243	339	355	8.2
Real Remuneration — Total Working Personnel	144	185	187	4.0
Total Real Incomes of the Population	191	256	262	6.2
Per Capita Real Incomes	171	220	223	5.1

Source: Romanian Government

ROMANIAN ECONOMIC INDICATORS

	M.U.	1970	1975	1980	1981
Fixed Assets (end of year)	thous. million lei complete inventory value	757.1	1,203.3	1,864.2	2,018.7
Volume of investments[1]	thous. million lei	80.0	137.7	210.5	208.0
Social Product[1]	thous. million lei	523.4	863.7	1,250.9	1,438.1
National Income[1]	thous. million lei	212.1	361.9	508.7	530.7
Industrial output[2]	thous. million lei	307.2	586.9	936.1	909.0
Building and Assembly Output[1]	thous. million lei	44.3	61.7	92.2	97.5
Gross Agricultural Production[1]	thous. million lei	68.6	93.8	129.1	179.3
Volume of Foreign Trade	thous. million lei foreign currency prices	22.9	53.1	110.0	332.4[3]

1 Data for 1970 and 1975 are expressed in 1963 comparable prices, those for 1980 regarding the volume of investments, the building and assembly output and the gross agricultural production in prices prevailing on January 1, 1977, those regarding the social product, the national income and the industrial output in prices prevailing at the beginning of the relevant year, while those for 1981 in current prices.

2 Data for 1970, 1975 and 1980 refer to the gross output, while those for 1981 to the marketable output.

3 Thous. million lei prices.

Source: Romanian Government

ROMANIAN NATIONAL BUDGET

(million lei)

	1950 1	1965 2	1975 3	1980 4	1981 5
Income of which	19,965.3	96,953.7	238,553.3	298,004.2	280,342.4
Turnover Tax	8,510.2	28,701.2	42,135.5	39,420.1	34,933.4
Profit Pymts. of State Enterprise and State Economic Organizations	3,189.4	20,683.4	45,538.8	82,976.9	81,929.4
Taxes and Other Pymts. from Socialist Units	5,785.4	25,885.4	91,427.1	21,427.1	20,808.5
Duties and Taxes from Population	1,420.5	5,672.2	20,200.9	2,956.2	3,216.4
State Social Insurance Income	1,059.8	5,930.5	17,198.0	32,323.7	34,740.3
Expenditures	19,073.2	93,057.3	236,168.6	296,787.3	271,823.2
Financing of the National Economy of which	10,009.1	63,494.6	155,827.7	185,080.5	162,137.6
— Science	—	1,436.0	3,166.8	4,867.8	5,602.4
Financing of Social and Cultural Actions	3,444.9	20,925.0	50,915.9	70,977.5	74,353.5
National Defense	3,246.4	4,734.9	9,713.2	10,393.6	10,502.5
State Power, Administration and Political Bodies, Bodies Subordinated of the Attorney's Office	1,491.9	2,285.2	2,673.9	3,439.9	3,657.0

Source: Romanian Government

AGRICULTURE

The varied natural conditions within Romania are reflected in the diversity of its agricultural pursuits.

About a third of the country is covered by plains that are well suited to agriculture. One third is taken up by hilly areas at an average altitude of 1300 to 1600 feet, with slopes usually sufficiently mild to allow most types of agricultural cultivation.

The rest consists of the mountainous areas which have supported a heavy agricultural population since prehistoric times, containing surfaces suitable for use as arable land as well as natural Alpine pastures.

Agrarian

Although Romania has traditionally been an agrarian economy, the current 5-year plan reemphasizes the importance of agriculture to the economy.

For the past 20 years, the major emphasis of economic growth in the Romanian system has been on development of heavy industrial, capital intensive projects. As a result of recent financial problems and the worldwide recession, however, the Romanian authorities have renewed their emphasis on the agriculture. Nowadays Romania actively solicits cooperation agreements in various fields of agricultural technology.

Exports

Unlike the consumer products area, where export sales may not yield hard currency, Romania believes that its climate and huge farm population put it in a good position to be a major exporter of agricultural commodities.

It is clear, however, that many portions of the agricultural sector are inefficient and unproductive by international standards. Therefore, renewed emphasis has been placed not only on the production of food products but on processing, transportation, and even packaging.

The Romanian government is understandably sensitive about the fact that it has an economy which can produce world-class electric generating equipment but lags behind in agriculture. As this program has a political as well as economic backing and has been emphatically endorsed by the government, Western agribusiness may find Romania a lucrative and fertile area for expansion.

Grains

The climate and relief of the extensive Romanian plains are favorable to the development of cereal crops. By the early 1980's wheat covered some 5,700,000 acres; maize, 8,200,000 acres. Cereals are also found in the sub-Carpathian region and in the Transylvanian Tableland, where they occupy a high proportion of the total arable land. Other cereals include barley, rye and oats.

PRODUCTION OF AGRICULTURAL COMMODITIES

(1000 metric tons: 1980)

Barley:	2,500
Corn:	11,200
Potatoes:	4,100
Cabbages:	1,000
Onions:	304
Tomatoes:	1,300
Sugar (raw value):	509
Sunflower seed:	817
Soybeans:	448
Linseed:	40
Plums:	620
Apples:	414
Grapes:	1,313
Tobacco:	39
Peas:	15
Beef and veal (live weight):	611
Pork (live weight):	1,106
Timber (1000 cubic meters 1980):	4593
Wheat	6,500

Vegetables

Vegetables are grown in a relatively small area (some 475,000 acres). Peas are the predominant crop; being capable of an early harvest, they allow a second crop usually of fodder plants to be grown on the same ground. Vegetable cultivation is particularly marked around Bucharest; there is specialization in the production of early potatoes, tomatoes, onions, cabbages and green peppers. Similar peripheral areas are found around Timisoara, Arad,Craiova, Galati, Braila, and other cities. The most important potato-growing area in the country is found in the Brasov and Sibiu, Harghita, and Mures districts. Other related crops include sugar beets (475,000 acres); sunflowers (10,300,000 acres) mostly on the Danube, Tisa and Jijia plains. Hemp, flax, rapeseed, soybeans and tobacco are also grown.

Viticulture

With some 750,000 acres under cultivation, Romania is one of the major wine producing countries of Europe. It specializes in the production of high quality wines, using modern methods, and with the growth of the tourist trade, it is becoming known to a wider international public. Large quantities are exported annually.

The major vineyards are at Odobesti, Panciu, Nicoresti, with a half dozen or more major centers. Both white (Grasa de Cotnari, Riesling, Tirnave, Murfatlar) and red (Pinot Noir, Babeasca, Sauvignon, Chardonnay) wines have won international awards.

Fishing

The river network of Romania, its lakes—especially the complex around Razelm—and its Black Sea coastal regions provide the basis for a well-developed fishing industry. The largest quantity of fish is obtained from the Danube and its delta and about 80% of the annual catch is consumed fresh. The canneries that process the remainder are located at Tulcea, Constanta, and Galati.

Livestock

Animal breeding has a long history in Romania, with the major stress being made on sheep breeding. The availability of grass, whether it be in the Alpine pastures or the Danube plain and valley, has been the major factor facilitating sheep raising.

LIVESTOCK

(January 1981)

(1000)

Cattle:	6,485
Sheep:	15,865
Pigs:	11,542
Horses:	566
Poultry:	97,800

MANUFACTURING

Iron and Steel

In recent years the Romanian iron and steel industry has been actively engaged in a much needed modernization process. One mill is over 212 years old.

The largest plant at Hunedoara has been modernized and extended and the number of blast furnaces increased; the new steel works, a rolling mill and a battery of modern coke ovens were also added.

Another integrated iron and steel plant was recently built at Resita and a tube mill at Roman. The capacity of the smaller mills at Otelu Rosu, Calan, and Cimpia Turzii and Calarasi was increased and a sheet mill built at Galati.

In the late 1960's and early 1970's more than half the pig iron and 5/7ths of the steel came from plants erected since 1950. Production of specialty steels has been increased with the completion of the new Galati and Tirgoviste Combines. By 1980 annual specialty steel production was 1.37 million metric tons.

The Romanian steel industry has recently adopted some of the most modern steel-making technology including continuous casting, large BOF furnaces (180 MT) with direct reduction in 40 minutes, two heavy rolling mills for plates with capacity of 4,000 millimeters and 10 cold rolling mills.

The Romanian iron and steel industry produces a full range of mill-forms with all surface preparations. The steel industry emphasizes oil country goods, flats, rebars, wire, bar, both hot and cold drawn, and tubes.

It is also capable of producing a full range of specialty steels including stainless, tool steel and high speed tool steel, made into various mill forms including wire, cord and electrodes. All forms of treatment can be performed on both specialty and carbon steels including heat treatment, sizing and cold rolling.

As a centrally planned economic unit, the Romanian iron and steel industry is both vertically and horizontally integrated, contributing substantial funds to research and development of its installations and production. It also incorporates R&D and production in such ancillary activities as coal products, coking and production of graphite electrodes (also available for export).

Non-Ferrous Metals

The non-ferrous metallurgical industry in Romania, although relatively new, is currently producing a wide range of industrial products. Aluminum production currently includes sheet coil, aluminum foil and electrotechnical aluminum (5 microns minimum).

The ferroalloy industry, primarily located at Tulcea, produces a full range of ferroalloys including ferrosilicon, ferromanganese, ferrochrome, etc. Production is almost sufficient for domestic consumption and there is some export availability of major ferroalloys.

Chemical Industry

The chemical industry, particularly the petrochemical sector, is one of the fastest-growing industries in Romania. Research and development in the petrochemical area dates back for many generations; it has only been within the last two decades that the Romanian chemical industry has been able to successfully utilize the fruits of indigenous R&D.

Although Romania was an importing country before World War II, the chemical industry has now been developed to the point where it exports substantial amounts. Chemical and petroleum products currently account for more than 25 percent of the country's overall exports.

In 1982, Romania produced more than 700 varieties of chemicals and was one of the 10 largest chemical-producing countries in the world. The current 5-year plan calls for increasing chemical exports substantially. Chemicals together with machine building and light industry, are expected to account for 64 percent of the country's exports by 1985.

Romania possesses most of the raw materials necessary for a highly diversified chemical industry (salt, natural gas, crude oil, coal, timber). It currently produces a wide range of plastics, synthetic rubbers, artificial fibers and yarns, chemical fertilizers and plant regulators, pesticides, biostimulators, pharmaceuticals, dyes, sodium and chlorosodium products, sulphuric acid, carbide and detergents. The Romanian chemical industry now supplies over half of all Romania's basic chemical needs and is expanding rapidly. The current 5-year plan places particular emphasis on this industry, already the largest of any communist country outside the Soviet Union. Western investment, coproduction, and joint ventures are actively sought in this area.

Romania's major fertilizer works are located in Navodari, Roznov, and Fagaras; factories for sodium products at Govora and Borzesti, and for manmade fibers and plastics at Savinesti.

Although Romania remains a major chemical importer, the current 5-year plan anticipates an increasing degree of self-sufficiency. Major targets for self-sufficiency include chemical and biochemical intergetics technology, alternative energy sources (biomass and catalytics).

Also included in this area are organic pigments for textiles, detergents, etc. Foreign technology is actively sought in these areas. Rubber and elastomer is currently beyond the R&D stage in Romania and substantial production is anticipated. Romania hopes to be net exporter of synthesized rubber products in the immediate future.

Romania's emphasis upon the research and development, particularly in the chemical industry, is coordinated by the National Council of

INDUSTRIAL PRODUCTION
(1,000 metric tons — 1980)

Hard Coal:	8,100
Lignite:	27,100
Coke:	3,033
Crude oil:	11,500
Natural gas (thousand cubic meters):	28,156,000
Electricity (kw – hr):	67,486,000
Cement:	14,607
Bauxite:	700
Iron ore (26% metal content):	2,333
Pig iron:	9,012
Crude steel:	13,175
Petroleum products:	24,700
Sulphuric acid:	1,756
Caustic soda:	723
Fertilizers (nutrient content nitrogenous):	1,707
Phosphate:	687
Cotton yarn (1979):	175
Cotton fabrics (square meters):	748,000
Wool yarn (1979):	71
Woolen fabrics (square meters):	128,000
Manmade fibers (1979):	205
Paper:	633

Science and Technology, presided over by Dr. Helena Ceausescu, wife of President Nicolae Ceausescu and a noted chemist in her own right.

Machinery

Romania is one of the major machine-building countries of the world. This industry is highly developed and accounts for more than 34 percent of the total industrial output of the country, about 80 percent of the quantity of investment equipment and more than a third of all exported goods.

Romanian machinery has an excellent reputation for quality and reliability. They have devoted considerable resources to new technology, particularly numerical controls (robotization). The backbone of the Romanian machine-building industry, however, continues to be heavy industrial equipment, tractors, turbines and large castings.

The machine-building industry offers a comprehensive list of products with more than 35 specialized plants turning out a wide range of machine tools, most of them with numeric control (nc) viz.: heavy turning and boring mills with a diameter of 5,000 millimeters to 16,000 millimeters; parallel lathes in the 1250 millimeter-2500 millimeter diameter range; horizontal boring and milling machines with a broach diameter of 160 millimeters, 200 millimeters, 240 millimeters, and 300 millimeters; machining centers with horizontal and vertical spindles; jig boring and grinding machines; slide grinding machines with a work width of 1,000 millimeters to 2,000 millimeters; gear grinding machines with worm wheels, etc. Romania currently produces over 384 types of machine tools, and due to heavy current investment, this variety is expected to increase to 655 by 1985.

Romania's fine mechanics industry is also highly diversified. Under the current 5-year plan, precedence is being given to measuring and control instruments which rely upon computer control and production of instrumentation for technological processes.

Major products include machine tool measuring devices, control apparatus, apparatus for dimensional and nondimensional control of standardized elements; remote transmisson and recording apparatus, microscopes, industrial robots, optic and electronic weighing apparatus, high precision micro reducers; programming mechanisms; (interior-exterior) numatic calibrating devices ; precision electric contacts, industrial anti-vibrating devices with electric or magnetic contact; pressure relays; industrial clockwork devices; medical research equipment; industrial and educational laboratories.

Electrical Equipment

As part of its diversification in the machinery area, the past two 5-year plans and the current 5-year plan (1980-1985) emphasize the development of the electrical equipment industry. This industry developed in recent years mostly with a view toward import replacement.

Romania currently produces almost all of its domestic needs for electric motors, consumer electronics and electrotechnics. In the past several years, it has developed a sophistication and is now capable of producing electric and electronic assemblies compatible with high speed computers.

The enterprises which operate under the auspices of the Ministry of Electrical Equipment employ almost 400,000 people. Currently, the production of electrical equipment goes primarily to other Romanian industries and exports are not as great as might be expected (about 20 percent of total production).

This sector is highly innovative; about 89 percent of the entire production will be new products compared with 1981. Penetration of the U.S. market has been minimal, although for several years they have had a U.S. representative. Romania produces electric motors from microsize (0.025 hp) to heavy industrial (2,000 hp). Romanian electronics have been fully integrated into printed circuit technology and numeric control.

One of the major developments in the past two years and one which will be emphasized in the current 5-year plan is transformer production. Within the next 18 months, Romania will become one of the few countries in the world producing grain-oriented silicon steel for use in large power stations.

The Romanian electronics industry also produces a wide range of consumer products including coffee grinders, hair dryers, vacuum cleaners, mixers and hand tools. Although most of these products currently go to Romanian and other CMEA markets, they can be modified and upgraded to satisfy the requirements of Western importers. The electronics industry in Romania is particularly anxious to enter the "private label" market in the United States at prices competitive with those offered by Asian suppliers.

Although Romanian computer technology lags far behind that of the West in terms of hardware, Romanian software, particularly for mechanical engineering applications is "state of the art." Major computer languages are FORTRAN and COBOL and mechanical engineering software programs have achieved modest success in Western markets. Romanian prices in this service area are remarkably low by world standards.

Handicrafts/Glassware/Ceramics

Despite its (well-deserved) reputation for producing shoddy consumer goods, Romania does manufacture some products which are of genuinely superior quality.

In handicrafts, crystal and ceramics, Romanian quality is as proficient as it is in the heavy industrial area for machine tools and petrochemicals. Romanian needlepoint and handicrafts (particularly silk-stitched blouses and shirts) are world-renowned. Romanian crystal, although not as well-known as Irish or Czech counterparts, is of equivalent quality.

Romanian ceramics are less well-known not due to their lack of quality, but to a dearth of Romanian marketing skills. These items are, along with wine, the major consumer bargains in Romania. None have established adequate markets in the West. They represent a major untapped resource of the country.

Lumber and Furniture

The lumber industry represents a very old tradition in Romanian economic life. In recent decades, the emphasis has switched from production to wood processing and the government has attempted to conserve the forest resources of the mountain areas.

In addition to the processing complexes at Blaj, Tirgu Jiu, and Pipera-Bucharest, a number of furniture factories have been erected at Targu Mures and Braila.

The main products of the lumber and furniture industry are timber, furniture, chipboard and fiberboard, veneer and plywood. The current 5-year plan provides for further development of this industry mainly by increased industrial processing of wood and wastes.

Footwear

The Romanian footwear industry is ancient, going back several centuries. Currently, major Romanian exports to the United States are not exactly modeled in *Vogue;* they consist mostly of high-quality work boots and shoes. The footwear industry, however, is highly sophisticated and can produce a wide range of (relatively fashion-insensitive) products such as hunting boots, work shoes, hiking and sporting footwear, and related accessories. Romanian prices for these items are low by international standards. Romania produces virtually all shoes necessary for domestic consumption and is a substantial net exporter.

Textiles and Apparel

The textile and apparel industry supplies all of Romania's domestic needs with enough available for substantial exports. Romania manufactures a variety of fabrics, knitwear, garments and leather products and increasingly relies upon synthetic fibers and yarns partially to reduce imports of natural fibers. The main centers of production are Bucharest, Oradea, Lugoj, and Timisoara.

Engineering

Most Romanian needs are now satisfied at home, and in some categories there is a surplus for export. The engineering industry produces advanced kinds of oil-drilling and mining equipment, tractors, lathes, turbines and electrical apparatus.

The Romanians are justifiably proud of domestic engineering projects. Although architecture can hardly be cited as a strong point of Romanian technology, heavy construction engineering is a standout. Romanian engineers and construction firms fill all Romania's domestic requirements and are currently active in a dozen overseas projects. Major areas of expertise include canals, road building, bridges, railroads, power plants and dams.

In recent years, the Romanian authorities have emphasized offshore infrastructure development projects and are actively seeking foreign partners in this area.

Romanian engineering crews in third countries are generally paid at rates a fraction of those offered by American companies doing business offshore. Third country joint ventures can be extremely attractive to foreign entrepreneurs. Further, the ordinary rules of joint ventures in Romania are at least negotiable with regard to third country projects. Depending upon the specific project, it might be possible for an overseas company to subcontract to Romanian engineering entities and still maintain control of the overall project.

Given the fact that the Romanian authorities are actively seeking such cooperation, it would seem propitious for foreign companies seeking to sell their products to third world countries to enter into cooperation agreements with Romania. Foreign suppliers for third country projects are also actively solicited by the Romanians for their offshore projects. Contacts with regard to these projects should be made through the Ministry of Foreign Trade.

Consumer Goods

By the late 1970's, the consumer goods industries had increased more industries' in line with the five-year plans announced by the government.

By the late 1970's, the consumer goods industries had increased more than 18 times since World War II. Ceramic and tile works, textiles, readymade clothing, leatherwork, footwear and metal consumer goods have all been extended. Several sugar refineries were built, including large ones near Cluj and Suceava; the number of food canneries increased, and large mechanized dairies were set up in Bucharest, Constanta, and Bacau.

In the Romanian system, consumer goods are assigned a much lower priority than major industrial goods. As a state-controlled economy, Romanian consumer goods are sold under monopoly situation. Those goods sold only locally often suffer from lack of quality and even availability.

Locally-made goods of export quality are available only in limited quantities at home. Although Romanian industry is capable of producing a wide variety of consumer products of world-class quality, these only become available on the Romanian market if an enterprise receives substantial offshore orders justifying the creation of product lines meeting international standards.

Examples of areas in which Romanian enterprises are actively seeking substantial export participation are consumer electrical goods (electric hand tools, kitchen appliances, etc.), and consumer electronics (radios, television sets, etc.).

Joint ventures, coproduction and licensing in the consumer products area would be well-received if there were a substantial export potential to third country markets. This, in turn, would give access to Romanian market which currently would not justify the commitment of resources for many of these product lines. Romanian industry, however, currently produces many of these products and is capable of building most of them to order. Romania actively solicits participation in the "private label" market and will make consumer goods to specification. Prices for such products are competitive with those produced in Asia.

MINERAL RESOURCES

The Romanian iron industry has strong bases in Hunedora, Resita, Galati, Bucharest, Iasi, Braila, Roman, and a number of other centers and has been of key importance in the industrial development of the country.

The nonferrous metallurgical industry dates back to the Dacian-Roman period. It is largely concentrated in the northwest and west of the country with copper, gold and silver production still active. Aluminum production is a relatively recent development. Alumina works at Oradea and Tulca supply raw material for the big aluminum complex at Slatina in the Olt district. Small quantities of lead, mercury and zinc are also produced.

Coal

Although coal resources include a number of categories — bituminous coal, brown coal and lignite — whose quality varies from region to region, the largest reserves are those of bituminous coal; a large part of Romania's bulk coal production comes from the Petrosani Depression alone.

Reserves of lignite, although of lesser quality, have been tapped in recent years to meet energy-producing requirements. With the exception of the Baraolt-Virghis Basin which lies within the Carpathian Range, most deposits are found along the fringe of the mountain areas.

Although coal production continues to increase marginally in Romania (1981 production: 36.7 million tons), stocks are sufficient for the foreseeable future. Nevertheless, there is a strong interest in alternative sources of energy, especially nuclear and hydroelectric power and offshore gas and oil exploration; some success has been achieved to date in discovering new Black Sea sources.

Gas and Oil

Oil deposits are found in the flysch, or thick, soft sandstone formations that run in a broad bend along the outer rim of the Carpathians and through the sub-Carpathian regions. Such centers as Ploiesti, Buzau, and Vilcea have long been famous for their oil-producing industry and they have been joined in recent years by production in the Plain of Ilfov. Natural gases — mainly methane — are produced in the center of the Transylvanian Tableland, and gases produced as byproducts of the oil industry are of increasing importance.

Romania's resource base of petroleum and natural gas is rapidly depleting. In 1976 Romania became a net importer of crude oil, but it continues to export refined oil products.

Chapter 3

INFRASTRUCTURE

SHIPPING

River transportation is important in Romania as the Danube criss-crosses the country for 1,075 kilometers. Romania also has 245 kilometers of coastline on the Black Sea. In 1980, 2350 million metric t/km of merchandise and 79,000,000 passenger/km were transported by river and 80,000 million t/km of merchandise by sea.

Inland water transport was enhanced with the completion of the Danube-Black Sea canal between Cernavoda and Constantia in 1983. In late 1983 construction began on a new Bucharest-Danube canal.

Ports

Romania, like the Netherlands, serves as a major entrepot trade port for most of Eastern and Central Europe. Lying at the delta of one of the major rivers of Europe, Romanian ports serve Yugoslavia, Hungary, Austria, Czechoslovakia and even parts of Switzerland.

MAJOR ROMANIAN PORTS

Black Sea

- Constanta
- Mangalia
- Sulina

Danube

- Orsova
- Drobeta-Turnu Severin
- Purnu Magurele
- Giurgiu
- Oltenita
- Calarasi
- Hirsova
- Braila
- Galati
- Tulcea

A canal linking the Danube to the Black Sea across Dobruja, between Cernavoda and Agigea-Constanta (40 miles/64 km.), was completed recently.

Inauguration of the Danube-Black Sea Canal by President Ceausescu

AIR TRANSPORT

Air transport is handled by two companies: TAROM (Transporturi Aeriene Romoine) and LAR (Liniile Aeriene Romaine).

There are 16 airports for domestic air traffic. Romanian companies also operate 36 overseas routes. Three international airports (Bucharest, Constanta and Timisoara) provide flight services for foreign companies.

Romanian Airlines

In 1981 Romanian airlines accounted for 2,362,000,000 passenger kilometers and 81.3 million net kilometer-tons of commercial freight.

Overseas

Romania is well connected with other major points in Europe and overseas. Airlines maintaining regularly scheduled service include: Aeroflot, Air France, Alitalia, AUA, British Airways, CSA, El Al, Interflug, JAT, KLM, LOT, Lufthansa, Malev, Sabina, SAS, Swiss Air, and Tapso.

Pan American World Airways discontinued flights two years ago, but has announced its intention to consider reopening its Bucharest office.

Airlines

AEROFLOT
35, N. Balcescu Blvd.; Bucharest
Telephone: 16 74 31

AIR FRANCE
35, N. Balcescu Blvd.; Bucharest
Telephone: 13 95 52

ALITALIA
41, Magheru Blvd.; Bucharest
Telephone: 59 75 20

AUA
7, N. Balcescu Blvd.; Bucharest
Telephone: 14 12 21

BRITISH AIRWAYS
22, N. Balcescu Blvd.; Bucharest
Telephone: 16 30 22

LOT
41, Magheru Blvd.; Bucharest
Telephone: 59 25 75

LUFTHANSA
18, Magheru Blvd.; Bucharest
Telephone: 12 99 50

MALEV
Otopeni International Airport
Telephone: 33 31 37/526

PANAM
4, N. Balcescu Blvd.; Bucharest
Telephone: 13 63 61

SABENA
24, N. Balcescu Blvd.; Bucharest
Telephone: 15 12 26

CSA
3-5, Batistei St.; Bucharest
Telephone: 14 80 59 and 16 47 05
Otopeni Airport
Telephone: 33 31 37

INTERFLUG
31, Soseaua Kiseleff; Bucharest
Telephone: 33 23 62; Telex: 11-565
Otopeni Airport
Telephone: 33 31 37/521

SWISSAIR
18, Magheru Blvd.; Bucharest
Telephone: 13 66 76

Diesel engine manufacturing at Resita

ROAD AND RAIL

In 1980 Romanian railways stretched 6,905 miles (11,110 km.); 46.8 km. of track for every 100 square km. of territory. The rail system is extensive for a country its size and reaches all major population centers.

Rail network

Romanian railways provide the main transportation for both goods and passengers in the country. The national rail network focuses on such large industrial centers as Brasov, Cluj, Arad, and Ploiesti, although the rugged terrain of much of the country also influences routes. In recent decades diesel and electric engines have been placed in service and the major links have all been electrified.

Road transport

By 1980 the total length of public roads in Romania was 45,596 miles (73,364 km.); (30.9 km./100 square km.). Of this, 34,054 km. were paved. In 1980, Romania had 450,000 passenger vehicles and 300,000 commercial vehicles.

Auto assembly line

COMMUNICATIONS

In 1980, Romania's 5,121 post offices handled 884 million letters, 1,526 million newspapers and periodicals, 14.6 million parcels, 42.2 million surface and air mail deliveries and 5.4 million cables. In 1980 there were 1.6 million telephone subscribers and 192 cities were connected to the inter-city autonomous telephone exchange.

Local telephone service is fairly automatic and dependable. International telephone and telegraph connections are generally good but delays may occur when placing calls.

New apartments at Bucharest

ENERGY

One of the greatest problems facing Romania in the aftermath of World War II was the backwardness of the national electric power industry. Major plans spanning 1951-1960 supplemented by two later plans have resulted in a substantial rise in power output.

Projects

Foundations for this progress were a series of gigantic power projects, each of which has a 100 megawatt or more capacity.

Foundations for this progress were a series of gigantic power projects, each of which has a 100 megawatt or more capacity.

The most important projects have been those at Singeorgiu de Padure; at Bicaz, on the Bistrita River; the Gheorge Gheorghiu-Dej station on the Arges; and the enormous Iron Gate project on the Danube (a joint Romanian -Yugoslav project).

POWER GENERATION

(Million Kilowatts)

	Total	Thermoelectric Power	Hydroelectric Power
1950	2,113	1,944	169
1965	17,215	16,210	1,005
1970	35,088	32,315	2,773
1977	59,858	50,513	9,343
1979	64,933	53,595	11,138

Chapter 4

FINANCE

FINANCING

For the past few years, Romania has undergone a significant crisis in both balance of payments and balance of trade. By mid-1982, the International Monetary Fund (IMF) and Romania agreed upon an adjustment program within the framework of the 1981 stand-by agreement.

This program has already resulted in a partial recovery from the prior financial difficulties which severely supressed Western sales to Romania since the third quarter of 1981.

The Romanian authorities are extremely zealous in implementing the austerity and efficiency-improving measures agreed upon with the IMF and the country is currently ahead of its payment schedule. Although the pace of improvement in Romania's fiscal/monetary status has been gradual because it depends upon the completion of private and public reschedulings and the restoration of business confidence in the country, the recovery has been faster than anticipated.

Decline

Romania's financial and economic problems resulted in a substantial decline in U.S. exports from $332 million in the first five months of 1981 to $142 million in the same period of 1982 and a sharp drop in U.S. imports from $235 million to $160.7 million in the same period.

Import curbs and declining real investment which were down 7 percent in 1981 continue to restrict the market, although there was some improvement in the 4th quarter of 1982 and the 1st quarter of 1983. Romanian demand is strongest for supplies depleted over the past 24 months including raw materials, spare parts, and other items required for export production.

Through the 2nd quarter of 1983, many suppliers of these goods were owed payments for earlier shipments. The Romanian Foreign Trade Bank began authorizing payments to clear old debts and most of the older obligations have now been liquidated. The goal of reducing the prior current account deficit put intense pressure on Romania's foreign trade enterprises to export, and they are now legally required to maintain the planned balance in their trade transactions.

Further, Romanian importers have been squeezed to cut all unnecessary imports and production of items for import substitution has been reemphasized. The apparent current account surplus has been achieved largely by rolling back imports to austerity levels — particularly in the consumer area — and pushing exports — particularly those destined for hard currency countries.

Counterpurchase

The Romanian demands for 100 percent counterpurchase will, therefore, probably persist indefinitely. Despite the added complexity, many firms have found countertrade a way to continue doing business without becoming entangled in Romania's cash flow difficulties. While confirmed letters of credit remain scarce, countertrade commitments with fixed delivery dates are relatively low in risk. The preferred barter arrangement is one in which the Romanians ship first.

Recovery

Presuming the financial recovery program proceeds, there is hope for the mid-to-long range. Romanian authorities have acknowledged that unwise product specialization choices and quality problems led to poor performance in Western markets. Over the past two years, there have been significant shake-ups in the Romanian foreign trade bureaucracy and President Ceausescu has made extraordinary public statements in recent times acknowledging errors and promising that "corrections" would be made.

To date, the Romanians have met or exceeded all the conditions laid down by the IMF and foreign bankers. Their publicly (and privately) stated objective in the short term is to restore foreign bankers' confidence in Romania's ability to pay its debts.

This, they say, goes hand in hand with restoration of foreign business confidence in the Romanian market as a growth area. To date, they have partially succeeded in the former and seem to be going all out to encourage substantially increased trade. In early January, 1983 Romania's financial authorities requested rescheduling of 70 percent of their 1983 debt service.

They also requested rescheduling of the official debt for 1983. This postponed payments of about $1 billion due to Western banks and governments.

The recent disbursement of a $325 million tranche of a three-year IMF standby credit, together with a $1.8 billion hard-currency trade surplus in 1982 stemming largely from a strict curtailment of imports, gave Romania much greater flexibility in managing its economy. Romania declared itself committed to continue the IMF adjustment program. An important element in this program, import limitations, especially on foreign agricultural purchases, will continue.

Controls

Strict controls on investment will remain with emphasis being placed on completion of unfinished projects under the 1983 annual plan. While this temporarily precludes some contract negotiations for major capital goods sales, Romanian companies have again begun approaching suppliers of technology for raw material recovery, energy efficiency, agricultural modernization and food production.

Sales prospects are currently best for raw materials, spare parts, chemicals and coal. Following a severe drop in exports from $504 million in 1981 to only $224 million in 1982, both imports and overall trade recovered remarkably in 1983.

BANKING

Romania's banking system, as in the other East European countries, is a state monopoly that exercises centralized control over both the domestic economy and foreign trade.

The National Bank of Romania (NBR) exercises the functions of a central bank and, together with the Ministry of Finance, sets the foreign exchange rate, establishes foreign exchange budgets, and decides on the distribution of exchange balances among various currencies and depositories.

RBFT

Subordinate to the National Bank is the Romanian Bank for Foreign Trade (RBFT). Although the two banks interchange personnel, the Bank for Foreign Trade is primarily responsible for payments related to international trade and service transactions.

The services available include: confirmation of letters of credit, endorsement of bills of exchange, payment against shipping documents, discount of commercial paper, credit guarantees, purchases and sale of foreign currency, and other commercial activities. The RBFT may also conclude agreements with foreign banks concerning financial transactions and accounting practices. The RBFT maintains correspondent relationships with hundreds of banks worldwide and has a fair credit rating in world financial circles. The RBFT also provides foreign exchange facilities for tourists, diplomats, and visiting businessmen.

As a CMEA member, Romania is also a member of the International Bank for Economic Cooperation (IBEC) and the International Investment Bank (IIB), independent entities located in Moscow. Although these banks can provide short, medium and long-term financing to member countries, their activities in Romania are traditionally minimal.

State Control

In Romania all banking and insurance institutions are state controlled. The former National Bank of Romania was nationalized on December 20, 1946 and all private banks on June 11, 1948. The Romanian Banking System is an adjunct of Romania's centrally-planned fiscal and monetary policies. In addition to traditional banking activities, the banking system of Romania executes redistribution of funds temporarily available in the economy by granting credits, organizes and pays discounts (without cash) for economic and socialist organizations, pays for state budget appropriations, finances capital construction, offers foreign trade discounts, and organizes credit operations of foreign countries.

The Romanian banking system comprises the following:

The National Bank of the Socialist Republic of Romania

The National Bank is the chief link of the banking system, issuing and circulating currency, executing the state budget, and supervising the implementation of the financial credit and currency policy, non-cash discounts and loans to socialist units.

Investments Bank

This institution finances, credits, and discounts investments for state-owned economic units and those of the handicrafts cooperatives, consumer cooperatives and public organizations.

The Bank for Agriculture and Food Industry

This bank credits, finances and discounts production, investments, and goods circulation in agriculture, the food industry and water management.

The Romanian Bank for Foreign Trade

This is the institution most frequently encountered by foreign businessmen. It makes payments, credits and supervises the exchange of currency and related operations with foreign countries.

The Loans and Savings Bank

This is the equivalent of a central savings and loan institution. It deposits temporarily available money from the population, credits other links in the banking system, grants loans to individuals for home construction etc.

Insurance in Romania is exclusively handled by the State Insurance Administration which issues compulsory and voluntary insurance, for individuals and corporations.

EXCHANGE CONTROL

Foreign visitors entering Romania may bring with them any amount of foreign currency. Romanian currency may also be brought in but only if it has been delivered to the tourist by the banks of East European countries which have received the corresponding amount in lei from the National Bank of Romania. Export of lei in cash are prohibited.

While in Romania, foreign visitors may exchange currency only at the foreign trade bank or other authorized bodies. Foreigners changing currency must ask for an exchange voucher which will enable them to prove, on leaving the country, that all transactions have been done legally. This voucher entitles them to reconvert the unspent lei into hard currency.

Visitors should be aware, however, that tourists are generally required to spend the equivalent of $10 in hard currency each day in Romania, unless traveling on a prepaid, all-inclusive tour. Visitors should carefully retain receipts for all money exchanges and purchases to present on departure.

Trading

Romanian trading entities must apply to the Foreign Trade Bank to obtain the convertible currency necessary to pay for imports. The terms of payment are established in the sales contract concluded with foreign firms.

Payment can be made by documentary letters of credit, payment on receipt of the documents, simple transfer or any other method used in banking practice. In putting letters of credit into effect, Romania usually applies the rules of the "Uniform Customs and Practice for Documentary Credits" of the International Chamber of Commerce.

Black Market

Like almost all Eastern European countries, there is a thriving black market in Western currency. To say that the authorities disapprove of street transactions in lei, however, would be an understatement.

There are severe criminal penalties for such transactions. The "entrapment" defense is definitely *not* an option in Romanian courts. The risk is hardly worth the small profit that might be made in such illegal transactions.

TAXES

Foreign trading firms and economic organizations which open agencies in Romania must pay annual taxes on their net income. These taxes are calculated in terms of remuneration by consignment by the firms they represent or annual taxes according to the listed number of employees they have which are listed with the Financial Administration of the Municipality of Bucharest. Tax liability advice can be received from the ARGUS bureau.

Treaty

The so-called Convention Between the Government of the United States of America and the Government of the Socialist Republic of Romania with Respect to Taxes on Income, which came into effect in February, 1976 is designed to avoid double taxation of business, personal service and investment income.

American citizens may credit most taxes paid in Romania against their U.S. income tax. Tax rates on interest and royalty income are reduced.

The treaty also assures non-discriminatory treatment by providing that citizens and businesses of one country will not be taxed more in the other country than are the host country's own citizens and businesses.

CURRENCY

The Romanian currency is the leu (plural lei). The currency is decimal; 1 leu = 100 bani. The leu has been fixed to the price of gold since 1954; 1 leu = .148122 grams fine gold.

This valuation, however, is primarily for international valuation purposes. There is no free gold market in the country. The National Bank of Romania issues currency in denominations of 10, 25, 50 and 100 lei bills and 5, 15, 25 bani, 1 leu, 3 and 5 lei coins.

Dual

There is a dual exchange rate for currency which is periodically fixed: the "official" rate and the "non-commercial tourist rate." The leu does not "float" for exchange purposes within Romania but is established by the government. The "official" rate is established primarily for international monetary purposes. It is rarely, if ever, used for computing valuation for commercial purposes. The non-commercial rate accounts for almost all of the hard currency transactions in Romania.

Fluctuations

These rates are periodically adjusted by the National Bank to reflect both fluctuations in values of Western currency and the relative strength of the Romanian economy, and to accomplish other monetary goals, including increasing the current account balance. Most international trade is, however, conducted at the non-commercial rate.

Since the monetary crises of the late 70's and early 1980's, the Romanian monetary authorities have been extremely conservative in making adjustments to the leu's valuation. Since it is illegal for Romanian citizens under most circumstances to hold hard currency, it is unnecessary for the Romanian monetary authorities to "defend" the lei in the traditional Western sense. They do, however, tend to maintain a rough parity with Western currencies.

Chapter 5

INVESTMENT

FOREIGN INVESTMENT

More than 200 foreign firms have established branch offices or joint ventures in Romania over the past decade. These range from Dow Chemical to a half dozen Lebanese firms.

About half of the American companies doing business in Romania today do so through their European subsidiaries.

Although the Romanian government does not keep accurate statistics on the dollar amount of foreign investment in that country, reasonable estimates range upward of $2 billion.

Listing

A complete listing of foreign companies doing business in Romania can be obtained from PUBLICOM, 22 N. Balcescu Boulevard, Bucharest, Romania.

Chemical equipment factory, Bucharest

JOINT VENTURES

There are currently five major industrial joint ventures in Romania with Western firms. One of them, Rom Control Data (RCD) is an American venture established approximately a decade ago. The others involve major Western European firms.

One of the major advantages of a joint venture in Romania is that all sales *within* Romania can be made for convertible currency. Therefore, the issue of exchange control (i.e. conversion of lei into hard currency) does not arise.

For these transactions, since they are almost exclusively with governmental or semi-governmental agencies, the books of the joint venture corporation are kept in dollar or other convertible currency denominated accounts.

Thus, the sometimes laborious central bank approval for transferring funds offshore is short-circuited and profits can be repatriated on the same basis and with the same alacrity that they would if the Romanian operation were West European subsidiary.

In joint ventures, as with other types of business activity engaged in by Western firms in Romania, the government encourages export sales, particularly to West European and other hard currency countries.

Some Western companies entering into joint ventures in Romania find it desirable to have their Romanian operations perform activities or produce products which are being phased out of their larger operations in the West. Given the substantial Romanian government investment, denominated in dollar terms and always more than 50 percent, smaller scale operations in Romania can be justified than would ordinarily be a reasonable financial proposition in the West.

The Romanian government is particularly anxious to acquire skills, know-how and manufacturing capability of a wide variety of high-technology equipment such as computers, office machinery, scientific machinery and equipment.

Motivation

Romania's motivation for promulgating the joint venture decrees are to obtain foreign technology, management, marketing expertise, and capital; to develop joint research activities; to improve the country's trade position by import substitution, export stimulation and diversification; to gain access to marketing networks of the foreign partner and develop collaboration of their markets; and to fulfill domestic industrial needs.

To encourage foreign companies to enter joint ventures, Romania permits the foreign party to repatriate its profits and allows its participation in the management of the venture.

The Romanian party usually offers a reservoir of trainable or trained labor and may provide access to local material resources, other socialist country markets and markets in some developing countries.

Romania favors joint ventures that include one or more of the following characteristics:

- Projects requiring substantial fixed capital investment or advanced technology unavailable locally. Such projects are often aimed at industrial sectors such as electronics, where Romania lags technologically behind the West.

- Projects for the manufacture of goods that fulfill home market needs and would otherwise have to be imported.

- Export-oriented projects that upgrade local goods or raw material and provide the venture with positive convertible currency balance.

Perhaps most important, the proposed joint venture must conform to Romania's so-called five year development plans.

In industries where Romania already possesses technology and know-how and where complementary technical assistance is desired, other types of industrial cooperation agreements such as coproduction and licensing are preferred by the Romanian authorities.

Labor-intensive joint ventures are not encouraged. Projects involving the local manufacture of components to be incorporated in foreign-made products are also not encouraged because of concern that such projects would be affected by market cycles and put the centrally planned Romanian economy in a vulnerable position.

CMEA

Joint ventures with Romanian entities are not necessarily the best means of entering other CMEA member countries. Under Romanian law, all joint venture transactions must be conducted in convertible currency. While this has the advantage of easy repatriation of profits, it limits the competitiveness of the joint venture's exports to other CMEA countries.

For high technology companies which, however, rely on constant improvement of their products, a joint venture may provide markets within CMEA that can be adequately serviced (at least initially) by some of the company's less advanced technology and products.

This provides the company with an additional return on existing technological assets.

Gradual

Some foreign investors might wish to take a gradual approach by initially considering less complex forms of doing business. These include *coproduction* agreements where one of the parties provides subassemblies or manufactured parts which are in turn assembled into a final product by the other party, payment occuring either in terms of product in cash; *licensing;* or construction of a *turnkey* plant.

These less complicated forms of cooperation avoid the problems arising from intimate long-term collaboration in an unfamiliar business environment.

Following the successful implementation of such limited cooperation efforts, an American company could then escalate its involvement to the level of a joint venture. Romanians are generally receptive to this gradual approach since it allows the parties to adapt to each others' business perspective and to establish viability of their targeted markets.

Success

The success of a joint venture also depends on a number of other factors. These include local business climate, the potential of the targeted markets and the effect of competition. Also important are the form of association, quality of management and the parties' concurrence in business objectives.

Complexity

Although Romania has publicly stated its desire to attract more Western capital, the complexity of Romanian laws, regulations and long-term economic planning regarding the activities of the joint ventures have discouraged many American corporations from engaging in this activity.

Given the current trends in Romania's foreign trade policy, however, the Romanian authorities are more receptive to this type of arrangement and will interpret their laws to fit their current needs. In particular, Romanian authorities have publicly advocated expediting joint venture arrangements in the areas of medium-technology goods.

Philosophy

Perhaps one of the most important reasons for the dearth of joint ventures in Romania relates to differing philosophical concepts with regard to profits. In Romania and other CMEA economies, profit is viewed mainly as return on capital investment rather than as a blend which includes return on resources such as R&D management, technical services, marketing and a return for the adjustment necessary in existing or planned capacity. Another basic conceptual difference encountered in Romania is a lack of distinction between risk capital and assumed loans to be supplied to a joint venture by the foreign party.

According to some Western businessmen, some Romanian planners, in their pursuit of rapid industrialization, fail to adequately evaluate the impact of new technology and products on their own economy, the potential of targeted markets, and the economies of scale of proposed manufacturing plants.

It is important to recognize that Romanians (and East Europeans in general), operate primarily under the risk of penalties, not rewards; they are not risk takers or entrepreneurs, but perform under strict guidelines established by central planners. (See also CONDUCTING BUSINESS)

Further, Romanians because of the structure of their economy sometimes do not appreciate that foreign firms must justify the company's business performance to stockholders and the stock market.

In Romania, the state finances, owns and operates all enterprises and gears its economic planning to 5-year cycles from which the annual plans are derived. This difference, which affects profit policies and corporate planning, has restricted the field of prospective joint venture investors to companies which can afford the luxury of long-range planning in exchange for a permanent foothold in the Romanian market.

Long-Range

Despite all these drawbacks, joint ventures or other forms of cooperations between Romanian and foreign firms can be profitable under many different circumstances. Short-term profits, however, can rarely be achieved in the Romanian context by a joint venture. An overseas investor interested in short term profits would be well-advised to enter into direct contractual relationship for the supply of Romanian goods. In the medium term foreign companies would be generally best served by coproduction arrangements. In the mid to longer range, however, a joint venture arrangement has significant advantages, not the least of which is the ability to repatriate profits in dollars at the discretion of the company rather than that of the Romanian authorities.

OPENING AN OFFICE

Romanian law sets a number of preconditions for the establishment of a corporate office in Romania.

A license is required for opening an agency and is issued by the Ministry of Foreign Trade and International Economic Cooperation after approval by the Council of Ministers for a two-year period which may be extended upon request of the firm.

To obtain a license the following documents must be filed with the Chamber of Commerce and Industry (in the ARGUS office) by the foreign firm:

- An application (filed on a special form by the ARGUS office) for the opening of the agency including the functioning of the agency, the wages and foreign currency of the Romanian staff to be hired, the number, functions, addresses of the foreign citizens to work with the agency, enumeration of the property the firm intends to bring to Romania.

- The Romanian foreign trade companies with which the firm maintains trade relations.

- A receipt acknowledging the payment of the stamp duty and license charge (the current stamp duty is 21,600 lei). This amount should be paid in foreign currency to the Foreign Trade Bank (account no. 63.02.00) of the Financial Administration of the People's Council of the Municipality of Bucharest. In the event the license is issued for a period of more than two years, the firm must pay the tax difference in foreign currency for this period *pro rata*.

- A certificate issued by the Chamber of the Commerce of the country of origin showing the firm applying for the license has legal status in that country and stating the object of its activity and capital.

- A certificate from the bank handling the financial details of the foreign trading firm or economic organization testifying to its reliability.

- A certificate of incorporation, deed of partnership, etc. or any other certificate certifying the legal existence of the firm in the country of organization.

- A power of attorney by which the firm empowers its representatives to act on its behalf, including details as to the limits of their competence.

All the above documents in the original language should be filed and an authorized translation into Romanian filed with the ARGUS office simultaneously with the application. This translation into Romanian may be obtained from the Romanian Embassy in the country of origin of the applicant firm or at the State Notary Office in Bucharest.

Application

At the time the application is filed, the applying firm must write a letter to the Chamber of Commerce and Industry of Romania to the attention of the ARGUS office, asking that it recommends to the Ministry of Foreign Trade and International Economic Cooperation permission to open an agency. This letter must specify the objectives of the firm in the Romanian market.

The license which is ultimately issued under the above procedure will note the place where the functions of the agency are to be carried out, the objectives of the office in Romania and the conditions under which it is to function. The license is valid for two years and can be extended upon request.

If the above license application procedure appears complex, it is. The ARGUS office, however, will assist a foreign firm in completing all necessary applications in a timely manner at a small fee.

The licensed agency of the company must register with the Chamber of Commerce and Industry which will provide building or office space through the CARPATI National Travel Office. The agency must also register with the Financial Administration of the Municipality of Bucharest and register its transport vehicles within 15 days after the license is issued. Again, ARGUS will assist the foreign corporation with these formalities at a modest fee.

LOCAL CONTENT AND OWNERSHIP

As a state-controlled economy, Romania does not permit local production of goods by companies wholly owned by foreign corporate entities.

Further, a complex system of licensing and approvals encourages the highest possible percentage of local content of any product made in Romania.

Foreign joint ventures must, *from the onset,* be majority-owned by Romanian state institutions.

Capital

Not only does this decrease the control which a foreign entity can assert over their Romanian partner, it also reduces capital requirements.

It is important, therefore, to have a very clear understanding of the operation and relationship of the parties before active investment commences.

The amount of local content and coproduction agreements is not a matter of law but rather negotiation in a contractual context.

Generally, the Romanian authorities favor contracts which provide for an increasing percentage of locally-produced components for a finished product over a period of years.

LABOR

The Romanian labor force is highly trained by world standards. As a newly industrialized country, Romania has a preponderance of workers in the productive as opposed to the service sector.

EMPLOYED POPULATION — STRUCTURE BY BRANCHES OF THE NATIONAL ECONOMY

(end of year/thousand persons)

	1965	1975	1980	1981
Employed population total	9684.0	10150.8	10350.1	10375.5
Industry	1862.9	3109.7	3678.7	3748.6
Building	609.3	825.5	857.6	797.8
Agriculture	5476.5	3837.4	3048.1	3002.8
Forestry	18.8	26.5	39.5	36.2
Transport	296.7	431.8	629.3	658.2
Telecommunications	52.2	68.7	79.9	82.9
Movement of Goods	386.4	558.7	619.9	619.6
Local Husbandry of the Housing Estate and Other Non-Productive Services	205.5	348.7	390.9	397.6
Education, Culture and Art	341.1	408.6	430.5	435.5
Science and Scientific Services	50.8	77.3	98.3	106.5
Public Health, Social Assistance and Physical Culture	188.6	267.3	281.7	285.8
Administration	98.8	67.6	64.8	64.5
Other Branches	96.4	123.0	130.4	139.5

By 1980, more individuals were employed in industry than in agriculture and the relative shift is likely to increase in the future.

PERCENTAGE OF TOTAL	1965	1975	1980	1981
Industry	19.2	30.6	35.5	36.1
Building	6.3	8.1	8.3	7.7
Agriculture	56.5	37.8	29.4	28.9
Forestry	0.2	0.3	0.4	0.4
Transport	3.1	4.3	6.1	6.4
Telecommunications	0.6	0.7	0.8	0.8
Movement of Goods	4.0	5.5	6.0	6.0
Local Husbandry of the Housing Estate and Other Non-Productive Services	2.1	3.4	3.8	3.8
Education, Culture and Art	3.5	4.0	4.2	4.2
Science and Scientific Services	0.5	0.8	0.9	1.0
Public Health, Social Assistance and Physical Culture	2.0	2.6	2.7	2.8
Administration	1.0	0.7	0.6	0.6
Other Branches	1.0	1.2	1.3	1.3

Unions

Like all Socialist countries, Romania views labor unions in an entirely different context than the West. According to Communist dialectic, the workers are the owners of all the means of production and therefore, "confrontational" labor-management problems are superfluous.

In fact the labor unions in Romania are much like "company unions" in the United States. There are plant-level organizations which discuss grievances in which "management" participates. If the disputes are not resolved at the plant level, government-appointed arbitrators are often asked to intervene.

If the dispute continues, there is often direct intervention from the national level and it is not unknown for "management" officials or workers to be dismissed or transferred.

Strikes

Given this type of centralized control, strikes are unknown in Romania. On the other hand, Romanian workers are given effective life tenure upon hiring.

Romania, however, was one of the first countries in Eastern Europe to have a system of rewards and punishments to encourage better productivity.

The productivity gains in Romania, compared with its neighbors, attest to the success of this pragmatic approach. While it is still extremely difficult to dismiss an employee, the system incorporates methods of rewards and punishments for outstanding achievement (or lack thereof) which tend to ameliorate the deficiencies of a stridently Socialist system. This, combined with the relative freedom from industrial unrest, make the Romanian work force highly attractive to Western entrepreneurs.

Employing Staff

ARGUS can arrange for hiring Romanian personnel for a foreign agency and can refer those qualified for appropriate positions.

To hire a Romanian staff, the foreign enterprise must lodge an application with ARGUS specifying the necessary number of people, required qualifications and necessary languages. ARGUS will submit two or three proposals and the agency may select among them.

Foreign enterprises should be extremely careful in the initial hiring process, since once hired, it is extremely difficult under Romanian law to dismiss an employee.

Wages

Romanian wage rates are fixed by administrative decree and cover all levels from the top (director level) to bottom (doorkeeper, courier). Romanian law provides for numerous subcategories of job descriptions but, in general, these rates average about one-third of those in the United States.

Contracts

Employment contracts may be concluded for the period in which the operating license is valid or for shorter period and may be extended when the license itself is extended. Such contracts may be cancelled by mutual consent with 90 days advance notice. In this event, however, the ARGUS agency must be notified in writing. ARGUS itself may cancel the contract for abuse, but this provision is rarely exercised.

Travel by Romanian employees both domestically and internationally must be at the expense of the foreign firm's agency. Travel costs are drawn against the agency's account at the Romanian Foreign Trade Bank denominated in hard currency.

Chapter 6

TRADING WITH ROMANIA

TRADING

According to the Romanian Constitution, the country's foreign trade is entirely controlled by the state. This monopoly is carried out by the Ministry of Foreign Trade and International Economic Cooperation. This Ministry negotiates and signs agreements, conventions, protocols; facilitates trade and organizes Romania's participation in international economic organizations.

Romanian foreign trade law is relatively straightforward by American standards; virtually all relevant laws and regulations can be found in a pamphlet available from Publicom: *Romanian Foreign Trade Law.*

Romania's economic development has resulted in diversified international economic exchanges. In 1982, Romania maintained trading relations with 150 states.

ROMANIA'S FOREIGN TRADE

(million lei)

	1965	1970	1975	1980
Total	13,072	22,866	53,095	112,896
Export	6,609	11,105	26,547	53,890
Import	6,463	11,761	26,548	59,006

EXPORTS

PRODUCT	PERCENTAGE 1965	1970	1975	1980
— Machinery, equipment and transportation means	18.8%	22.8%	25.3%	26.2%
— Fuels, raw materials and metals	25.1%	22.7%	22.3%	29.5%
— Chemical products, fertilizers, rubber	6.4%	7.0%	10.8%	10.1%
— Non-edible raw materials	13.8%	10.2%	6.3%	4.6%
— Raw materials for food production	7.6%	4.5%	5.7%	3.9%
— Food commodities	13.9%	12.1%	10.6%	8.1%
— Industrial consumer goods	11.0%	18.1%	16.1%	15.5%
TOTAL	100.0%	100.0%	100.0%	100.0%

IMPORTS

PRODUCT	PERCENTAGE 1965	1970	1975	1980
— Machinery, equipment and transportation means	39.9%	40.3%	34.7%	24.6%
— Fuels, raw materials and metals	31.4%	30.4%	38.2%	50.3%
— Chemical products, fertilizers, rubber	6.3%	6.7%	6.5%	6.4%
— Building materials and auxiliaries	1.4%	1.5%	1.1%	1.0%
— Non-edible raw materials	11.1%	10.1%	8.4%	5.7%
— Live animals	—	0.2%	0.1%	0.1%
— Raw materials for food production	0.8%	2.3%	5.0%	5.7%
— Food commodities	2.4%	3.0%	2.2%	3.2%
— Industrial consumer goods	6.7%	5.5%	3.8%	3.0%
TOTAL	100.0%	100.0%	100.0%	100.0%

While Romania's major trading partners are "Socialist" countries, Romania has for the past 20 years resisted full CMEA integration and has proceeded with its own rapid and independent industrialization.

Purchases

Romania generally confines its purchases from the West to the technology, installations, equipment, products, and raw materials not locally available and necessary to carry out its 5-year plans.

ROMANIA'S CHIEF EXPORT PARTNERS IN 1980

(percent of total)

U.S.S.R.	18.7
West Germany	8.4
East Germany	5.6
Italy	5.5
P.R. of China	4.8
United States	3.9
Czechoslovakia	3.4
Poland	3.3
France	3.0
Holland	3.0

ROMANIA'S CHIEF IMPORT PARTNERS IN 1980

(percent of total)

U.S.S.R.	15.6
United States	7.4
Iraq	7.3
Federal Germany	6.4
Iran	5.2
P.R. of China	4.7
East Germany	4.5
Czechoslovakia	3.3
Libya	3.2

For a number of years, Romania has been the United States' largest trading partner in Eastern Europe, excluding the Soviet Union.

In 1982, trade with Romania slipped, primarily due to the severe economic slump facing that country. With the worldwide recovery in general, and Romania's recovery in particular, the trend seems to be reversing and bilateral trade increasing.

Romania is particularly anxious to reverse the trade "slide" and appears willing to make significant trade concessions to remedy this situation.

U.S. TRADE WITH COMMUNIST COUNTRIES

U.S. Domestic Exports (FAS)

(Millions of U.S. $)

	Total 1981	Total 1982	Jan-Mar 1982	Jan-Mar 1983
Albania	6.14	16.40	0.23	2.80
Bulgaria	258.10	106.45	37.30	15.67
Czechoslovakia	82.42	83.60	32.53	12.87
German Dem. Rep.	295.56	222.66	120.24	40.29
Hungary	77.51	67.84	21.63	21.40
Poland	680.55	292.61	39.00	71.35
Romania	503.89	223.23	91.12	52.24
Total East Europe	1,904.17	1,012.79	342.05	216.60
USSR	2,338.57	2,583.67	1,266.41	665.33
Total Communist Countries	4,242.73	3,596.46	1,608.46	881.93

IMPORT AND EXPORT CONTROLS

The Customs Code of the Socialist Republic of Romania governs customs formalities. All goods entering or leaving the country are subject to customs control at border points and inland customs checkpoints.

In general, all inbound goods are subject to duties at varying rates. Some exports are also subject to customs duties. These apply primarily to large quantities of goods (meat, etc.) being taken out of the country by individuals. Export duties rarely apply to commercial items.

The Customs Code in its entirety can be found in the pamphlet, *Romanian Foreign Trade Law,* issued by Publicom (Foreign Trade Publicity Agency), 22 N. Balescu Boulevard, Bucharest, Romania.

Customs formalities for business (both for imports and exports) are carried out by the Foreign Trade Organizations (FTO's) through the specialist company ROMTRANS.

Temporary Imports

Temporary exports and imports, samples, personal-use objects of Romanian and foreign travelers, and objects required by diplomatic and consular offices and their members are exempt from customs duties.

Should objects brought into or taken out of the country be of extremely high value or exceed their personal needs, however, they may be subject to duties. The same applies for objects introduced into or leaving the country by parcel post.

In the past five years, Romania has recognized the advantage of *foreign trade zones* and has established a major free port at Sulina. Romanian laws with regard to this foreign trade zone are essentially the same as those applying in the United States and Western European countries. Storage, trans-shipment, and even manufacturing can be accomplished in the Sulina free port upon application.

Non-Tariff Barriers

Romania does not maintain a discreet system of non-tariff barriers (NTB) such as the U.S. quotas on textile imports. In fact, the entire Romanian system is an NTB, since one must have a license to import any product.

Such licenses are issued by the Ministry of Foreign Trade (MFT). The MFT, in turn, will not issue licenses for import of goods not in conformity with the official 5-year plan.

All imported items are therefore "under quota" and it is important to have the cooperation of the MFT before any firm plans are made for importing products into Romania.

The MFT "quotas" are re-established every year and although they are not public information, the MFT will advise foreign businessmen of the likelihood of issuance of a license. Licenses are issued for a particular period of time (usually a calendar year) and may include other restrictions. These may be negotiated with the MFT.

Luxury Goods

In addition to licensing requirements, Romania also has strict controls with regard to many types of goods. Under current economic conditions it is highly unlikely that licenses would be issued to Romanian Foreign Trade Organizations for the importation of luxury consumer goods for general sale in the Romanian market.

"Luxury" goods in the Romanian context include such mundane items as portable tape recorders, cigarettes, whiskey, apparel, jewelry and books and periodicals.

These goods may, however, be imported into Romania (with the exception of certain types of literature) for sale in the so-called "convertible currency" stores.

Marking

Like all countries, Romania has an extensive set of laws relating to health, safety and marking requirements of imported consumer goods. In general, Romanian labeling, safety and health requirements are similar to those of the major Western European countries. These requirements vary, however, depending upon the nature of the product involved; specific provision should be made with regard to such matters in any contract negotiated with a Romanian entity.

Boycotts

While Romania has a cumbersome and elaborate export licensing system, it will sell almost anything to almost anybody.

Exceptions to this rule are exports to South Korea, Taiwan, and South Africa — countries with which Romania does not maintain diplomatic relations. No Romanian-made goods may be shipped directly to these countries and export applications to those destinations will be automatically rejected.

Foreign Controls

Export controls are imposed unilaterally on exports to Romania by the United States, and multilaterally through COCOM, which includes Japan and the 15 NATO countries, excluding Iceland.

SOCIALIST REPUBLIC

OF ROMANIA

SOCIALIST REPUBLIC OF ROMANIA
Municipality
Town
IAŞI
County Seat
Main Roads
Railways
County Boundaries
State Boundaries
0 15 30 45 60 km
THE BLACK SEA
BULGARIA
BOTOŞANI
SUCEAVA
IAŞI
NEAMŢ
BACĂU
VASLUI
COVASNA
VRANCEA
GALAŢI
PRAHOVA
BUZĂU
BRĂILA
TULCEA
IALOMIŢA
ILFOV
CONSTANŢA
Dărăbani
Dorohoi
Săveni
Siret
Rădăuţi
Solca
Gura Humorului
SUCEAVA
Cîmpulung Moldovenesc
Fălticeni
Hîrlău
Paşcani
Tîrgu Frumos
Tîrgu-Neamţ
Borsec
Topliţa
Bicaz
PIATRA NEAMŢ
ROMAN
Negreşti
Huşi
VASLUI
Gheorgheni
Bălan
Buhuşi
BACĂU
Moineşti
Comăneşti
MIERCUREA-CIUC
Vlăhiţa
Tîrgu Ocna
Slănic Moldova
GHEORGHE GHEORGHIU-DEJ
BÎRLAD
Băile Tuşnad
Bereşti
Adjud
Baraolt
Tîrgu Secuiesc
Panciu
Mărăşeşti
TECUCI
Covasna
Tîrgu Bujor
Odobeşti
FOCŞANI
Intorsura Buzăului
Săcele
Predeal
Azuga
Sinaia
Rîmnicu Sărat
GALAŢI
BRĂILA
Isaccea
Măcin
TULCEA
Sulina
Comarnic
Slănic
Vălenii de Munte
Breaza
Cîmpina
Plopeni
BUZĂU
Făurei
Boldeşti-Scăeni
Băicoi
Urlaţi
Mizil
Moreni
PLOIEŞTI
Babadag
Urziceni
Hîrşova
Ţăndărei
SLOBOZIA
Găeşti
Titu
Buftea
BUCUREŞTI
Feteşti
Cernavodă
Năvodari
CĂLĂRAŞI
Medgidia
CONSTANŢA
Videle
Techirghiol
Eforie
Olteniţa
ALEXANDRIA
GIURGIU
Mangalia
Zimnicea
Braţul Chilia
Braţul Sulina
Braţul Sf. Gheorghe
Siret
Prut
Moldova
Bistriţa
Trotuş
Ialomiţa
Argeş
R.
S.
26°
27°
28°
29°
30°
48°
47°
46°
45°
44°

These controls are designed to prevent the export of goods or technology which could make a significant contribution to the military potential of any nation when this would prove detrimental to the national security of COCOM members. Judgments are made on a transaction-by-transaction basis, and the United States regards these controls as a non-negotiable matter of national security.

Incidentally, Romania receives more liberal treatment from the United States in the application of these controls than many other communist countries.

CONTRACTS AND DISPUTES

Disputes arising from commercial contracts may be settled by arbitration if the parties have so stipulated in their contract or if the parties agree to resort to arbitration after the conclusion of the contract.

The International Commercial Arbitration Commission (ICAC), an independent body working within the organizational structure of the Chamber of Commerce and Industry, resolves disputes arising from foreign trade and economic, technical and scientific cooperation agreements between Romanian and foreign entities or persons.

The Arbitration Commission also adjudicates disputes arising from contractual relationships between joint companies established in Romania. It is governed by its own rules of organization and functions under the Civil Law Code.

COUNTERTRADE

Romania demands some of the highest countertrade (countertrade percentages per transaction) of any CMEA country (100 percent counterdelivery commitment may be initially requested from any western imports).

Whether such demands are met is determined during the negotiating process. The nature and priority of the imports together with bargaining often reduce the demand to lower percentages.

Guidelines

Specific guidelines may be provided by the various Romanian industrial ministries to the foreign trade organizations setting forth desirable countertrade goals in accordance with established annual export targets. Exceptions to countertrade obligations can be made, however, for extremely important deals.

Some foreign companies have found that certain Romanian products are offered in countertrade at inflated prices, and suffer from dubious quality and lack of after-sale service. Others, particularly in the heavy machinery field, have been generally pleased with Romanian goods.

Romanian authorities may seek to restrict counterdelivery commitments to the original importing Foreign Trade Organization (FTO) or the industrial ministry to which the FTO is responsible.

Romanian FTO's do give serious consideration to tying future imports to firm countertrade contractual obligations requiring the Western exporter to purchase a specified value of particular Romanian product within a year. The current practice is to require a contract which allows for a range of countertrade commodities "mutually agreed upon" by the parties expressed as a percentage of the western export contract.

Emphasis

Since the present emphasis is on increasing exports, Romanian FTO's might show some flexibility in enforcing the terms of the countertrade contract if the Western party runs into difficulty securing or disposing of the countertrade bids within the alloted time frame. The FTO's, however, will insist upon fulfillment of the countertrade obligations and are interested in securing the non-fulfillment penalties only as a last resort.

When confronted with countertrade demands and provided they agree to countertrade terms, overseas businessmen should first concentrate on the selection of goods that could be absorbed within their own company or by their clients. Foreign businessmen should be aware that the list of Romanian exports offered for counterpurchases may be years old and that many of these goods listed may be unavailable because of prior commitments or limited production. They may wish to use the services of an experienced trading house to dispose of the countertrade goods offered.

Available Items

The lists of items available for countertrade generally "track" the development plans. It is difficult to have additional items added to the countertrade list, but Romanian authorities will show flexibility within the list itself. In particular, generally-described items in the list may be customized to fit the precise specifications of a Western trader. Western businessmen should be sure to make their specifications clear or they will be given "off the shelf" items which may not be suitable for Western markets.

FINANCING TRADE

In addition to Romania's ability to finance imports and exports, the large commercial banks, located in the United States, Japan, and Europe, are the most important institutions in financing trade with Romania.

In the United States, commercial banks provide most of the short-term (up to 1 year) and medium-term (1 to 5 years) financing of East-West trade. This includes both suppliers' and buyers' credits.

Generally, U.S. banks do not extend long-term financing, though such financing may be available through a European bank to a European subsidiary of a U.S. firm.

Long-Term

Long-term financing for Romania is available from the Export-Import Bank of the United States (Eximbank) with the participation of commercial banks. A U.S. commercial bank, on behalf of a client, may also arrange long-term export financing through syndication with various European banks or financial entities.

A U.S. businessman seeking financing should start with his local bank, which in many instances can refer him to one of its large correspondent banks active in East-West trade.

Romania is the only communist country which permits foreign bank branches to operate within its territory. Manufacturers Hanover Trust Company of New York established a branch in Bucharest in 1974.

All foreign exchange activities of the Manufacturers Hanover branch are conducted under the supervision of the Romanian Foreign Trade Bank (RBFT). The branch performs many of the services customarily available at banks in the West.

PATENTS, TRADEMARKS, COPYRIGHT

Romania is a party to the "Paris Union" International Convention for the Protection of Industrial Property and subscribes to all its amendments. Non-Romanian inventors as well and their assignees are therefore entitled to the same treatment as Romanian citizens under Romanian patent law.

Foreign nationals have one year from filing the original application in their home country to preserve their patent priority by filing a corresponding application in Romania.

Patent Law

The current patent law in Romania is Law No. 62 of October 30, 1974, on Inventions and Innovations. It provides full protection for foreign technical processes applied in Romania and offers important incentives to Romanian inventors. It also stipulates tight controls and selective standards for purchasing inventions.

Romanian patent applications are filed with and awarded by the State Office for Inventions and Trademarks (OSIM), an agency of the National Council for Science and Technology (NCST). OSIM is headed by a director whose job is similar to that of the U.S. Commissioner of Patents and Trademarks. The OSIM staff is divided into sections of technology and science which recommend the allowance or rejection of patent applications.

Rejected applications may be resubmitted to an OSIM commission; decisions may be appealed to the courts. To file a patent application with OSIM, however, the foreign applicant must go through ROMINVENT, the Bureau of Foreign Patents and Inventions of the Chamber of Commerce and Industry. ROMINVENT acts as patent agent and attorney for all foreign nationals and legal entities to obtain patent protection in Romania.

Foreign applicants must provide ROMINVENT with the power of attorney in order to be represented before OSIM. ROMINVENT will provide a fee schedule to any foreign agent or attorney upon request.

Fifteen Years

Once granted, a patent is valid for 15 years from the date of registration with OSI. Once issued, a patent must be worked within three years from the date of issue or four years from the filing date, whichever is later. If not worked, the patent is subject to compulsory state license.

Patents give the patentee exclusive rights to the use of invention in Romania. A patent does not, however, confer upon one patentee the right to organize the production of the patented product in Romania or to import into the country. In Romania the means of production belong to the state, and the state maintains a monopoly over all foreign trade.

Romanian law actually prohibits Western companies from obtaining patents on certain types of inventions. Specifically, patents are granted only to socialist state organizations for the following: substances obtained by nuclear fission or chemical means; pharmaceuticals; means of diagnosis and medicinal preparations; methods for prophylaxis; food products and flavorings; strains of plants, bacteria and fungi; and new animal and silkworm breeds. Patents are obtainable on new and progressive technical solutions which can be used in the economy, science, national defense, or other parts of economic and social life.

Trademarks

Romania has joined the Madrid Arrangement Relating to the International Registration of Trademarks and has subscribed to all amendments of that arrangement. The current trademark law is Law No. 28 of December 29, 1976 on Trade and Service Marks and Brands.

As with patents, trademark applications are filed with OMSI through its intermediary ROMINVENT. Unlike patents, trademarks do not require prior registration in the owner's country. Trademark applications are examined by OMSI for their novelty and will be rejected if the mark is copied, annotated, deceptive or is not sufficiently distinguishable from other marks of the same goods.

Accepted trademarks are published; any opposition must be filed within six months of publication. Trademarks are valid for ten years from the date of application and may be renewed for the same period. There are 34 classes of goods and 8 classes of services for registration purposes.

A registered trademark vests exclusive rights of the owner and is enforceable by him against unauthorized use. Transfer or premature extinction of trademarks is handled through ROMINVENT.

Copyright

Romania is a member of the Berne Convention on Copyrights and the University Copyright Convention. The copyright law is Decree 321 of 1956 on Copyrights. The United States has a reciprocal copyright agreement with Romania.

LICENSING

For the past 15 years, Romania has actively sought Western licenses. Licensing agreements are common throughout the economy, particularly in the machine building and chemical/petrochemical sectors.

In recent years, however, the Romanian government has attempted to curtail its industry's expensive appetite for foreign licenses in favor of using Romanian research and design facilities.

Romania does not have a central licensing agency, but rather, negotiates license transactions through specialized staff in certain FTO's.

The major FTO's involved in licensing are:

Uzinexportimport (machine building)

Electroexportimport (electrical machinery)

Electronum (electronics)

Industrialexport (oil and gas extraction and processing)

Technoimportexport (medical and transportation equipment; instrumentation)

Romchim (chemical and petrochemical)

Romenergo (electric power)

Romconsult (consulting, export of Romanian licenses)

Where possible, Romania prefers to tie the purchase of a license to a cooperation arrangement whereby part, if not all, of the purchase is paid for in the resulting product. However, it has sometimes purchased licenses with no countertrade demands.

Chapter 7

CONDUCTING BUSINESS

GOVERNMENT ECONOMIC STRUCTURE

The Romanian economy is highly centralized and is, like other East European nations, based upon a system of planning — including five-year plans, annual plans, and foreign trade plans. This planning process is diversified and involves a wide range of organizations. Economic decisions are, however, taken at the highest levels of the government.

SCESD

Romania's top economic body is the Supreme Council of Economic and Social Development (SCESD) headed by the President. It is composed of both party and government officials and controlled by the Council of State.

The Supreme Council has an overall policymaking role together with the subordinate Central Economic Research Institute (CERI) which coordinates all Romania's economic research activities.

The Central Committee of the Romanian Communist Party (RCP) also has its own economic departments divided by economic or industrial sector. The party maintains control at all levels of the economy. Party bodies, for instance, establish guidelines for the Council of Ministers, which acts as the principal executive body for all questions relating to the economy.

Below these organizations, the economy is separated into economic/industrial ministries or "technical production" ministries. These ministries have broad responsibilities for their respective sectors.

Under these ministries are the industrial centrals which combine several enterprises and suppliers. These centrals oversee the actual producing units such as factories and enterprises.

MFT

The Ministry of Foreign Trade and International Economic Cooperation (MFT) formulates the annual foreign trade plan in coordination with the technical-production ministries, which are responsible for overall planning in their respective sectors.

The MFT then monitors and guides implementation of the Plan. It also insures import and export licenses to other government agencies and staffs and foreign trade offices.

In its role as promoter of Romanian exports, the MFT is also involved in trade fairs and foreign exhibits.

In a 1973 reorganization, a Directorate for Cooperation was established within the MFT, and increased cooperation activities with western firms had become a primary goal of the ministry.

Technical-Production Ministries

In trying to understand the industrial structure of Romania, one should look at the system as if each technical-production ministry were a western-style conglomerate. In this context, the senior officials of a ministry are equivalent to senior operating officers of the various industrial centrals, research and design institutes, and foreign trade organizations whose activities are subordinated to this ministry.

The various ministers of the technical-production ministries are, in effect, the board chairman of the companies under them. Generally speaking, the most important subunits of such a ministry are the industrial centrals. Research and design institutes are also important. The Ministries have under their supervision foreign trade organizations, the equivalent of an import-export department in a western firm.

Industrial Centrals

Industrial centrals (IC's) are groups of enterprises or producing units having related products, functions, or structures under a single management. The IC's were established in the late 1960's as an attempt at economic decentralization. IC's have not become the semi-autonomous industrial organizations they were intended to be, but rather serve basically as large-scale production entities with somewhat limited authority and responsibility. They are subordinate to the technical/production ministries.

In foreign trade, IC's provide data and information to the ministry to which they are responsible for purposes of developing the foreign trade Plan. In some instances, IC's are also authorized to negotiate and sign contracts for trade transactions as well as cooperation arrangements such as joint ventures.

Research and Design Institutes

Research and design is centrally planned and controlled through the National Council of Science and Technology. Actual research and design is carried out by R&D institutes which are subordinate to the technical/production ministries. The number of such institutes has been expanded. They plan an important role in foreign trade planning and decision making.

Foreign Trade Organizations

Foreign Trade Organizations (FTO's) are "independent" economic units which receive part of their funds from commissions on transactions they conclude.

Each FTO deals with specific products, equipment or areas even though these sometimes may cut across ministerial lines. FTO's have wide latitude in choosing their foreign partners subject to review by the MFT and the applicable ministry whenever the contract is large.

They are authorized to sign contracts and other trade documents as principals, and may negotiate and conclude long-term contracts, re-export transactions, cooperation agreements, compensation deals and the establishment of equity joint ventures.

Enterprise and End-Users

Producing enterprises and factories cannot act as principals in foreign trade transactions and may not be open to direct contact with foreign firms. These enterprises, however, frequently provide information and advice to the appropriate FTO or industrial central. End-user representatives often participate in the negotiation phases of a contract. Enterprises which are not part of an industrial central are subordinated directly to the technical-production ministries.

Chamber of Commerce and Industry (CCI)

The Chamber of Commerce and Industry is a semi-governmental entity made up of more than 700 member organizations. It includes all of Romania's foreign trade entities and related economic and industrial organizations.

The Chamber provides information about Romania's economy, foreign trade system, and foreign trade laws and regulations. In addition, it promotes Romanian products abroad, arranges contacts between foreign producers and Romanian foreign trade entities, and offers a wide range of services and facilities designed to assist foreign businessmen. Its Foreign Relations Department handles inquiries from abroad and its Arbitration Commission assists in resolving disputes arising from foreign trade transactions.

OCM: Goods Control Office

The quality and quantity control of import, export goods is undertaken by the OCM or Goods Control Office. This agency carries out a wide range of operations. Upon request, the OCM will: perform quality control either piece by piece or at random; insure the control of perishable goods; draw samples; assist in the selection of goods loading and storage of products, etc.; conduct laboratory analyses; and control all means of transport. For each of its operations, OCM issues control certificates.

OCM services may be secured by permanent contracts or by special control orders submitted by mail, cable or telex. Generally, finished goods are presented for control but, upon request, control and testing may be performed at any stage of production. OCM serves as an "independent" testing facility performing services much like Underwriters Laboratories in the United States. In short, OCM through its technical staff and library acts as an agent for purchasers to assure the quality, packaging, service and shipping of any goods ordered from Romania. Its certificates may be submitted to financial institutions as a precondition for the payment of letters of credit as per contracts between Romanian and foreign companies.

ARGUS

ARGUS is perhaps the most important Romanian institution for foreign businessmen. Acting under the aegis of the Chamber of Commerce and Industry, the ARGUS office is empowered to represent foreign trading firms and economic organizations upon their request.

This agency performs the following functions on behalf of foreign principals:

- Trade operations at the conclusion of agreements such as placing and acceptance of offers and orders; delivery of offers to beneficiaries to obtain technical visas; contacts Romanian foreign trade companies;

- Monitors export and import contracts and insures Romanian foreign trade organization (FTO) adherence to contract terms;

- Facilitates marketing studies and programs;

- Contacts the Romanian foreign trade organizations and other bodies with a view to opening joint ventures, technical assistance, etc.;

- Negotiates and mediates countertrade arrangements and facilitates "customization" of countertrade lists.

- Expedites foreign firm utilization of the Sulina Free Port; and

- Provides foreign firms documentation and information with regard to other economic and trade activities.

State Insurance Administration (A.D.A.S.)

A.D.A.S. is the State Insurance Administration which insures export and import shipments. A.D.A.S. also insures the motor vehicles of foreign tourists and acts as an agent for foreign insurance companies.

National Travel Office (ONT-CARPATI)

ONT-CARPATI, the National Travel Office, organizes tourist activities and services in Romania and abroad and plans the promotion and development of tourism in Romania. ONT also handles the rental of office space and living accommodations for foreign businessmen.

National Council for Science and Technology (NCST)

The National Council is charged with fulfilling RCP policy in science and technology, including the coordination of all research and technological development. Imports of high technology products and licenses are subject to National Council approval.

Foreign Trade Publicity Agency (PUBLICOM)

PUBLICOM is a specialized publicity and advertising agency. Its main objective is to publicize Romanian exports through radio and television services, media advertising, outdoor and indoor advertising, displays of Romanian products and symposia.

PUBLICOM edits periodicals and numerous economic and commercial publications designed to keep foreign markets informed about Romanian economic achievements, Romanian foreign trade regulations, and the availability of Romanian products.

PUBLICOM can also provide services to foreign companies doing business in Romania through its contacts with over 150 magazines and daily newspapers. In fact, entire foreign marketing and publicity plans within Romania must be handled through PUBLICOM and its related branches.

PUBLICOM also publishes a number of periodicals designed for foreign markets. These include both product-oriented magazines such as *Foresta* and the *Romanian Journal of Chemistry* (see Bibliography) and informational booklets dealing with Romania's economic foreign policy, foreign trade regulation, economic units, etc.

The Vidraru Dam, Argesh River

COMTURIST

COMTURIST is the agency providing foreign visitors with hard currency goods that are generally unavailable for sale in lei. The main units of the COMTURIST network are found in the larger hotels of Bucharest and Brasov along the Black Sea coast and in other major tourist areas.

COMTURIST also has offices where goods may be delivered in fulfillment of orders denominated in foreign currency. In its network of shops, COMTURIST offers Western and Romanian-made goods such as textiles, handicraft, ceramics, crystal, cosmetics, Western cigarettes, imported clothing, furs, carpets, electrical household appliances and electronic apparatus, automobiles, and liquor. COMTURIST accepts various methods of payment all designated in hard currency:

- Cash payment including travelers checks, credit cards (Diners' Club, American Express) deposited at the pay desk of the agency in Bucharest or Brasov;
- Cash payment deposited for the account of the COMTURIST agency at the Romanian Bank for Foreign Trade, account no. 40.36.200-4;
- Money order (mail or telegraphic transfer order) to the COMTURIST agency, account no. 40.36.200-4, with the Romanian Bank for Foreign Trade;
- Checks to the order of the COMTURIST agency.

When payment is made by the two latter methods, the following data should be included:

- Sender's name and address;
- Payee's name and address;
- Destination of the amount with the specific information with regard to the goods chosen and address to which they are to be sent. Any amount sent to COMTURIST for purchase of goods should include:
- A commission of $0.50 for each order up to $25 and $1.00 for goods exceeding $25;
- Four dollars for packing and transportation expenses per parcel if the goods are to be sent to an end-user's address in Bucharest or to the nearest railway station (or post office for the rest of the country);

- A bank commission of 1% of the remitted amount. Should the amount be remitted by check, an extra commission of $0.10 per check must be included. These should be added to the list price of the goods.

The methods of payment listed here enable people abroad to order products which they wish to send to relatives or friends in Romania. A catalog of items offered by COMTURIST is available upon request. For durable goods, COMTURIST provides the usual guarantees according to the product, extending from 6 to 24 months from the date of purchase. For automobiles, the guarantee period is 6 months from date of delivery or 6,000 kilometers, whichever comes first.

ILEXIM

Ilexim is the Romanian entity designated as the purchaser and distributor of all foreign-published books and periodicals distributed in Romania. In effect, Ilexim is the "sieve" through which all Western periodicals must pass before they are distributed in the Romanian market. Some Western periodicals distributed by Ilexim are available only for hard currency, but a majority are available for purchase in lei. For the latter, Ilexim exercises very conservative control over content. It does not exercise prior editorial control but does have veto power over printed material, much as a public library in the United States may choose not to purchase books which it believes might be offensive to the local populace.

NEGOTIATING AND PRICING

Contacts between overseas firms and Romanian FTO's or IC's may be initiated by either side. Foreign entrepreneurs may take the initiative by:

- Contacting the Romanian Embassies or Trade Offices. While these missions do not take part in commercial negotiations or signed contracts, they are important sources of information and can be useful in initiating contact between Romanian trade entities and foreign firms;
- Writing or telexing directly the appropriate Romanian entity;
- Sending company representatives to Romania to meet with appropriate FTO and IC authorities;
- Participating in Romanian trade fairs and other trade promotion events in Romania;
- Arranging to meet with Romanian foreign trade officials who visit abroad. Information about such visits can be obtained from the Romanian Embassies and Trade Offices.

Negotiating

Certain factors should be kept in mind in early negotiations, especially by firms new to the market. The process leading to a signed contract is essentially the same whether a foreign company is negotiating a major or small project in Romania.

Normally, several bids are required for each transaction. Only written contracts are valid in Romania; therefore, Romanian negotiators place heavy emphasis upon extensive discussions of contract details.

As a result, negotiating sessions are unusually time-consuming and costly. Numerous persons may be brought into the discussions at various points. Representatives of the FTO, the Foreign Trade Bank, the end-user plant, Research and Design Institutes, and ministries concerned must be satisfied before a contract is signed. The Vice President of the FTO or head of the pertinent FTO department usually conducts the negotiations, which usually take place in Romania.

Unless the FTO is under pressure to complete the deal within a specified time period, talks are usually protracted and several visits to Romania may be required.

This is particularly true when the trading partners are dealing with each other for the first time or have had minimal prior contact. The Romanians are cautious about accepting new methods and suppliers. After confidence is established, negotiations on subsequent projects are likely to be less protracted.

A foreign company's chances of concluding a contract are better if its negotiators are of a sufficiently high rank and have authority to sign for the company. A personal working relationship developed with the Romanians can facilitate negotiations. For this reason, firms have often found it useful to have the same company representatives participate in each negotiating session.

Negotiations with each of the most promising bidders who have submitted preliminary proposals to the FTO are divided into two distinct phases — the technical and the commercial. During the former, project specifications are reviewed extensively and revised often to determine what best fulfills Romanian requirements. It is sometimes useful to arrange for Romanian technicians and negotiators to visit one of the overseas firm's plants.

Specialists

Because of the exhaustive format of the technical negotiations, the foreign firm's negotiating team should include qualified specialists who do not need to refer technical questions to the home office. The Romanian side generally consists of well-informed technical personnel including plant managers, product engineers, and Research Institute staff.

If the initial contact was made by the Romanian side, it is particularly important not to underestimate the technical abilities of the Romanian side. The Romanians will know precisely what they want, having gone through a laborious interagency qualification process and will instantly recognize technical shortcomings.

After technical agreement is reached, Romanian officials hold discussions with the bidders and appraise their bids. Commercial talks, which lead to final selection of one bidder, may be conducted with several firms at the same time to obtain the best terms available. These sessions focus upon the project's financial aspects including price, financing, penalty payments and a myriad of other subjects such as delivery schedules, arbitration and training of personnel. Additional Romanian officials, usually from the Romanian Bank of Foreign Trade and Central Planning Offices, may be brought into the talks.

Counsel

While foreign businessmen in Romania are free to choose their own counsel and agents in Romania, they are generally well advised to seek the recommendation of ARGUS before retaining the services of independent agents.

ARGUS maintains lists of appropriate attorneys and other agents for various purposes. Although selection of an agent without an ARGUS recommendation is permitted, much time and effort can be saved by going through this "appropriate" channel.

Pricing

A company's pricing strategy when negotiating with Romanians can range from very simple to extremely complex, depending upon the business proposal under consideration. The simplest case is selling an off-the-shelf item that has a standard price. The most complicated cases occur when products, technology, licensing, and technical assistance are all being included in one contract.

In the more complicated cases the Romanian buyer will try to get the seller to quote a firm price early in the negotiations. The seller should ordinarily delay quoting a final price as long as possible and preferably only after all other terms and conditions have been set.

Since this is not always possible, the seller, when quoting a price, should explicitly define what is included and what is not. This will preclude unforeseen costs such as living expenses for Romanian technicians sent abroad, pre-shipment inspections, additional expenses for the seller's technicians during technical assistance, and many other items.

During the price negotiation, the Romanian side will seek to obtain the maximum price reduction possible. If a firm price is agreed to early in the negotiations, the seller may find the buyer trying to add additional items or services to this price, thus achieving what amounts to a price reduction. The seller should have sufficient flexibility built into the price to allow for some reductions during negotiations.

Nevertheless, repeated discounts of substantial amounts will cause loss of credibility for the original offer. If possible, the seller should try to receive a concession from the buyer for this price reduction. The buyer will have a reasonable idea of what a fair price should be and may, in fact, be negotiating with other firms at the same time. It also is important for the seller to specify the time period for which the price remains valid.

Royalties

The pricing of technology and/or manufacturing licenses presents special problems. Romania and other East European countries prefer not to pay royalties on production but would rather pay a specific sum, sometimes over a period of years. In this case, the seller must assure a fair return.

Other factors to be considered in quoting a price are inflation forecasts for the contract period, interest rate differentials that may occur as a result of using certain financing methods, and the increased costs of marketing in Romania. This last factor is especially important because a marketing campaign is more expensive in Eastern Europe than in Western Europe.

In no case should a company agree to a price that will not provide the minimum return on investment that the company requires. A company should not count on recovering initial losses in future contracts. Each contract must be considered separately.

During the negotiations, some firms have found it advisable to provide their own interpreters who are familiar with technical details. Often interpreters supplied by the Romanians are not fully qualified to translate necessary technical terminology. The Romanian negotiators should be informed immediately of an interpreter's presence.

A flexible approach with well-considered alternatives in case of impasse is invaluable during the arduous negotiating sessions. Foreign firms have sometimes found that difficult points, left temporarily unresolved, can be taken up successfully in later negotiations. It is also advisable to note in writing and initial those items that have been agreed to each day to preclude attempts to reopen the same questions at subsequent sessions, although this may be unavoidable as representatives of different Romanian agencies join the talks.

STATISTICAL INFORMATION

For an American businessman who is used to having market research data and information instantly available, Romania can be frustrating. Consumer marketing studies are virtually non-existent and even such ordinarily straightforward matters as production statistics are sometimes difficult to obtain.

Official Romanian statistics, for example, are often expressed in terms of growth rates rather than in real numbers. One must recalculate each year from a base, if known. Official Romanian statistical tables are, however, readily available from PUBLICOM (Foreign Trade Publicity Agency) and Ilexim.

Statistics

While these statistics are generally accurate, one should exercise extreme care in analyzing them. Definitions used for different categories are not ordinarily specified and bases for comparison will change from year to year being expressed, for example, in either foreign currency or lei.

Foreign embassies in Bucharest usually have experience in interpreting the differences between Western and Romanian statistical methods, and can be of real assistance to businessmen in decoding numbers.

MARKETING

To speak of "Romanian marketing" is to coin a contradiction in terms. As a state-controlled economy, where consumer goods are generally produced and sold by a state monopoly, marketing in the accepted Western sense is superfluous. Commercial messages in the Romanian media are rare by Western standards. Further, there are few commercial billboards, signs, or other advertising media. Nevertheless, Western goods are widely known and some have even made significant inroads among Romanian consumers.

Despite some lack of marketing skills by Western standards, PUBLICOM, the Foreign Trade Publicity Agency, engages in a wide variety of promotional activities on behalf of foreign firms in Romania. PUBLICOM organizes many publicity events for foreign firms including technical lectures, displays of products, technical meetings, roundtables with Romanian and foreign participation, technical exhibits of products and operation, direct mail and public relations ventures and posters.

While lack of marketing skills may not be particularly important within Romania, given their economic system, a foreign businessman needs to take special care when marketing Romanian-made goods abroad. Romanian packaging and labeling are usually unsuitable for Western markets. Extreme care should be exercised, for example, in insuring accurate translations of operating instructions. The Romanians are fond of hyperbole and although many speak English fluently, their use of the language sometimes leads to questionable conclusions.

Fairs

One of the best ways to improve business contacts and promote sales in Romania is participation in specialized exhibitions, trade fairs, and trade seminars. These events are attended by FTO and Ministry officials, representatives of Research and Design Institutes, and end-users. Although these meetings are excellent opportunities for broad exposure to the Romanian market, sales result slowly from participation fairs, seminars and exhibitions. Romanian purchases are usually the culmination of months of hard negotiation.

The most important event is the Bucharest International Fair usually held in October. In addition, Romania sponsors numerous industrial exhibitions each year. Firms interested in more information or in participating in one of these shows should contact PUBLICOM, 22 N. Balcescu Boulevard, Bucharest; TELEX: 11374.

A foreign company desiring to participate in Romanian fairs and exhibitions should also contact the Enterprise for Fairs and Exhibitions (ITE). This organization stages every international fair and exhibition in Romania. It also organizes Romania's official participation in international fairs and exhibitions abroad.

VENALITY

One of the best indicia of whether it is appropriate for Western businessmen to invest in any country is the "venality quotient". Regardless of how a country describes itself (capitalist, socialist, scientific-socialist, communist, etc.), it is impossible for a Western-oriented enterprise to return a reasonable profit if there is widespread corruption.

If, for example, bribes are anticipated at every stage of the negotiation process and are a common method of doing business, it becomes difficult to accurately estimate the ROI since bribe "costs" are difficult to estimate. Although the system of "gratuities" is rather common in Romania, the governmental structure is largely free of high-level corruption.

Rare

"Grease" payments in the form of a carton of cigarettes, a bottle of whiskey, to have a corporate car repaired expeditiously are common; large-scale bid-rigging through payoffs to government officials is rare.

While companies may argue they have been denied advantages because of their failure to engage in underhanded practices, the more likely explanation in Romania is that the bureaucratic wheels turn slowly and that it is this factor, rather than a lack of engaging in shady dealings on the part of the foreign firm, which is usually the cause.

Romania's slow economic progress in some areas has been caused less by the corruption of its officials than by the complex system of authorizing and regulating business activities. In this respect, ARGUS can be extremely effective in expediting the resolution of corporate problems.

Although ARGUS charges a small fee, it effectively acts as an ombudsman for business and can usually settle most minor and intermediate-range problems.

Most ranking Romanian officials are extremely puritanical. Even the mere mention of a bribe can be counterproductive. Don't do it.

INDUSTRIAL CENTRALS

Grouped by industrial ministry or sector and including major imports and exports.

Metallurgy Ministry

CENTRALA INDUSTRIALA SIDERURGICA GALATI
(Iron and Steel Industrial Central, Galati)

Galati — Romanian, Galati County, Sos. Galati-Smirdan, Telephone: 930/31900; Telex: 51253, 51257

Ferrous metallurgy products: foundry coke, cast-iron, steel, thick and thin plates, zinc-coated sheet iron included; casting equipment, wire products, spare parts, bent sections and metallic structures.

CENTRALA INDUSTRIALA SIDERURGICA, HUNEDOARA
(Iron and Steel Industrial Central, Hunedoara)

Hunedoara — Romania, Hunedoara County, 8, Dr. Petru Groza St., Telephone: 957/12533; Telex: 32411, 32412

Ferrous metallurgy products: foundry coke, cast iron, steel, finished rolled steel, casting equipment, cast iron pipes, iron and steel castings.

CENTRALA INDUSTRIALA SIDERURGICA, RESITA
(Iron and Steel Industrial Central, Resita)

Resita — Romania, Caras Severin County, 1, Podul Inalt St., Telephone: 964/17211; Telex: 44214

Ferrous metallurgy products: foundry coke, cast iron, steel, finished rolled steel, thick and thin plates, railway rails, tires and thrust plates, track material, drawn bars, metallurgical equipment, wire products and spare parts.

CENTRALA INDUSTRIALA DE PRELUCRARI METALURGICE, BUCURESTI
(Industrial Central For Metal Processing, Bucharest)

Bucharest — Romania, 256 Muncii Blvd., Sector 3, Telephone: 27 59 45; Telex: 10862

Rolled and welded tubes, finished rolled steel, steel and copper wire, welding electrodes, drawn bars, wire products, bent sections, spare parts and metallurgical equipment.

CENTRALA INDUSTRIALA PENTRU METALE NEFEROASE SI RARE, SLATINA
(Industrial Central For Nonferrous And Rare Metals, Slatina)

Slatina — Romania, Olt County, 116, Pitestilor St., Telephone: 944/ 11900; Telex: 47218

CENTRALA INDUSTRIALA PENTRU PRODUSE REFRACTARE, BRASOV
(Industrial Central For Refractory Products, Brasov)

Brasov — Romania, Brasov County, 127 Carierei St., Telephone: 921/ 23966; Telex: 12307

Production of refractory bricks and products, chamotte, antishrinkage powders, carbon products, abrasive disks, various abrasive materials.

CENTRALA DE PRELUCRARE SI COLECTARE A DESEURILOR METALICE, BUCURESTI
(Scrap Metal Collecting And Processing Central, Bucharest)

Bucharest — Romania, 4, Theodor Aman St., Sector 7, Telephone: 14 75 90; Telex: 10937

Machine Building Industry Ministry

CENTRALA INDUSTRIALA DE AUTOCAMIOANE SI TURISME, BRASOV
(Industrial Central For Lorries And Motor Cars, Brasov)

Brasov — Romania, Brasov County, 5 Poenelor St., Telephone: 921/ 37222; Telex: 12204

Manufacture of motor vehicles.

CENTRALA INDUSTRIALA DE TRACTOARE SI MASINI AGRICOLE, BRASOV
(Industrial Central For Tractors And Farming Machinery, Brasov)

Brasov — Romania, Brasov County, 5 Turnului St., Telephone: 921/ 10422, 10423; Telex: 12311

Manufacture of tractors and farming machinery.

CENTRALA INDUSTRIALA DE UTILAJ TEHNOLOGIC, CHIMIC, SI RAFINARIL, BUCURESTI
(Industrial Central For Technological, Chemical, Equipment And Refineries, Bucharest)

Bucharest — Romania, 355-357, Calea Grivitei, Sector 8, Telephone: 65 50 90; Telex: 11250

Manufacture of technological chemical equipment.

CENTRALA INDUSTRIALA DE UTILAJ ENERGETIC, METALURGIC SI MASINI DE RIDICAT, BUCURESTI
(Industrial Central For Power And Metalworking Equipment And Hoisting Machines, Bucharest)

Bucharest — Romania, 104, Sos. Berceni, Sector 5, Telephone: 84 20 20; Telex: 10243

Manufacture of power and metal working equipment and hoisting machines.

CENTRALA INDUSTRIALA DE MASINI SI UTILAJE PENTRU INDUSTRIA USOARA, BUCURESTI
(Industrial Central For Light Industry Machinery And Equipment, Bucharest)

Bucharest — Romania, 170, Sos. Bucurestii Noi, Sector 8, Telephone: 67 40 30; Telex: 10873

Manufacture of light industry machinery and equipment.

CENTRALA INDUSTRIALA DE UTILAJ TEHNOLOGIC SI MATERIAL RULANT, BUCURESTI
(Industrial Central For Technological Equipment And Rolling Stock, Bucharest)

Bucharest — Romania, 256, Muncii Blvd., Sector 3, Telephone: 27 70 40; Telex: 10344

Manufacture of technological equipment, rolling stock and building equipment.

CENTRALA INDUSTRIALA DE RULMENTI SI ORGANE DE ASAMBLARE, BRASOV
(Industrial Central For Ball Bearings And Assembling Parts, Brasov)

Brasov — Romania, Brasov County, 96, 13 Decembrie St., Telephone: 921/20641; Telex: 12245

Manufacture of ball bearings, bearings and assembly parts.

CENTRALA INDUSTRIALA NAVALA, GALATI
(Naval Industrial Central, Galati)

Galati — Romania, 132, Pacii St., Telephone: 930/10800; Telex: 51293

Naval construction.

CENTRALA INDUSTRIALA DE MASINI UNELTE, MECANICA FINA SI SCULE, BUCURESTI
(Industrial Central For Machine Tools, Fine Mechanics And Tools, Bucharest)

Bucharest — Romania, 250, Muncii Blvd., Sector 3, Telephone: 27 60 30; Telex: 11464

Manufacture of machine tools, fine mechanics and tools.

CENTRALA INDUSTRIALA DE MASINI SI APARAE ELECTRICE, CRAIOVA
(Industrial Central For Electric Machines And Apparatus, Craiova)

Craiova — Romania, Dolj County, 144, Calea Bucurestiului, Telephone: 941/40061; Telex: 41234

Manufacture of electric machines and apparatus.

CENTRALA INDUSTRIALA DE MOTOARE SI MATERIALE ELECTROTEHNICE, BUCURESTI
(Industrial Central For Electrical Engineering, Motors And Materials, Bucharest)

Bucharest — Romania, 4, Sos. Garii Catelu, Sector 3, Telephone: 27 20 90; Telex: 10781

Manufacture of electrical engineering motors and materials.

CENTRALA INDUSTRIALA DE ELECTRONICA SI TEHNICA DE CALCUL, BUCURESTI
(Industrial Central For Electronics And Computing Technique, Bucharest)

Bucharest — Romania, 7-9, Sos. Fabrica de Glucoza, Sector 2, Telephone: 33 71 70; Telex: 10895

Manufacture of electronic equipment and computing equipment.

CENTRALA INDUSTRIALA DE ECHIPAMENTE DE TELECOMUNICATII SI AUTOMATIZARI, BUCURESTI
(Industrial Central For Telecommunications And Automation Equipment, Bucharest)

Bucharest — Romania, 18, Kalinin Blvd., Sector 2, Telephone: 33 00 90; Telex: 11462

Manufacture of telecommunication and automation equipment

CENTRALA INDUSTRIALA DE UTILAJ PETROLIER SI MINIER, PLOIESTI
(Industrial Central For Oilfield And Mining Equipment, Ploiesti)

Ploiesti — Romania, Prahova County, 121, Democratiei St., Telephone: 971/42051; Telex: 19278

Manufacture of oilfield and mining equipment.

CENTRALA INDUSTRIALA DE RAFINARII SI EROCHIMIE, PLOIESTI
(Industrial Central For Refineries And Petrochemistry, Ploiesti)

Brazi — Romania, Prahova County, Telephone: 2 04 00; Telex: 19343

Processing of crude oil and derivatives; production of petrochemicals, chemicals, and plastics.

CENTRALA INDUSTRIALA DE INGRASAMINTE CHIMICE, CRAIOVA
(Industrial Central For Chemical Fertilizers, Craiova)

Isalnita — Romania
Dolj County, Telephone: 13405, 13327; Telex: 41239

Production of fertilizers and other chemicals, lacquers and paints.

CENTRALA INDUSTRIALA DE MEDICAMENTE, COSMETICE, COLORANTI SI LACURI, BUCURESTI
(Industrial Central For Medical Drugs, Cosmetics, Dyestuffs and Lacquers, Bucharest)

Bucharest, Romania, 246, Ion Sulea Blvd., Telephone: 43 35 50; Telex: 11849

Production of medical drugs, dyestuffs, cosmetics, lacquers, paints, inks, soap, detergents and other chemicals, rubber and plastic articles, metallic structures, PVC consumer goods, tire retreading, packing glassware.

CENTRALA INDUSTRIALA DE FIRE SI FIBRE CHIMICE, SAVINESTI
(Industrial Central For Chemical Yarns And Fibres, Savinesti)

Savinesti — Romania, Neamt County, Telephone: 13000; Telex: 25246

Production of chemical yarns and fibres and other chemicals, rubber technical articles and consumer goods.

CENTRALA INDUSTRIALA DE PRODUSE ANORGANICE, RIMNICU VILCEA
(Inorganic Products Industrial Central, Rimnicu Vilcea)

Rimnicu Vilcea — Romania, Vilcea County, 1, Uzinei St., Telephone: 16100; Telex: 48271

Production of chlorosodium products, carbide and other chemicals, rubber and plastic articles, paints, domestic soap, and candles.

CENTRALA INDUSTRIALA DE PRELUCRARE CAUCIUC SI MASE PLASTICE, BUCURESTI
(Industrial Central For Rubber And Plastic Processing, Bucharest)

Bucharest — Romania, Popesti-Leordeni, Telephone: 83 41 40; Telex: 10276

Manufacture of tires, tubes and auxiliary products for the tire industry; manufacture of technical rubber goods and plastic goods manufacturing equipment, the required molds included; chemicals, metallic structures, castiron parts, glass craftware, mirrors, hand-made tufted carpets, textile ready mades.

CENTRALA DE UTILAJE, PIESE DE SCHIMB PENTRU INDUSTRIA CHIMICA, BUCURESTI
(Central For Chemical Industry Equipment And Spare Parts, Bucharest)

Bucharest — Romania, 112, Sos. Vitan, Telephone: 44 11 94; Telex: 11613

Manufacture of chemical equipment, spare parts, armature, prototypes, measuring and control apparatus, anticorrosion protection installations and devices, equipment for pilot stations, various chemicals; coordination of nationwide production of oxygen and argon; determination of working conditions in chemical units and prevention of occupational diseases; acceptance of chemical industry equipment, rubber and plastic articles, wood products, textile ready-mades, rubber vulcanization.

TRUSTUL CONSTRUCTII MONTAJE SI REPARATII IN INDUSTRIA CHIMICA, BUCURESTI
(Chemical Industry Construction, Erection And Repair Trust, Bucharest)

Bucharest — Romania, 112, Sos. Vitan, Telephone: 49 11 94; Telex: 11613

Erection-assembling and repair and other specific jobs in the field of the chemical industry; secondary industrial production linked with these works.

CENTRALA DE DESFACERE A PRODUSELOR PETROLIERE "PECO"
(Central For The Sale Of "Pec" Petroleum Products)

Bucharest — Romania, 11 bis, G1 Budisteanu St., Telephone: 13 38 10; Telex: 10739

Sale and transport of petroleum products by pipeline, tank wagons, and tankers.

Electric Power Ministry

CENTRALA INDUSTRIALA DE PRODUCERE A ENERGIEI ELECTRICE SI TERMICE, BUCURESTI
(Industrial Central For Electric And Thermal Power Production, Bucharest)

Bucharest — Romania, 16-18, Hristo Botev Blvd., Sector 3, Telephone: 13 26 20; Telex: 10156

Production, transmission and distribution of electric and thermal power in Romania.

TRUSTUL "ENERGOCONSTRUCTIA," BUCURESTI
("Energoconstructia" Trust, Bucharest)

Bucharest — Romania, 103-105, Calea Dorobantilor, Sector 1, Telephone: 79 60 20; Telex: 10179

Construction of thermopower stations, smoke stacks and flues, cooling towers, etc.

TRUSTUL DE CONSTRUCTII HIDROENERGETICE, BUCURESTI
(Hydropower Construction Trust, Bucharest)

Bucharest — Romania, 23-25, Dimitrie Onciul St., Sector 3, Telephone: 35 54 70; Telex: 10244

Construction of hydropower stations and complex hydropower systems, dams, tunnels, sluices, river harnessing.

TRUSTUL "ENERGOMONTAJ," BUCURESTI
("Energomontaj" Trust, Bucharest)

Bucharest — Romania, 103-105, Calea Dorobantilor, Telephone: 79 70 20; Telex: 11335

Assembling work for hydro- and thermopower stations.

TRUSTUL "ELECTRAMONTAJ," BUCURESTI
("Electromontaj" Trust, Bucharest)

Bucharest — Romania, 158, Calea Mosilor, Sector 3, Telephone: 16 63 30; Telex: 10271

Erection of electric power transmission lines and transformer substations.

Mining, Petroleum and Geology Ministry

DIRECTIA GENERALA AUTONOMA A PETROLULUI SI GAZELOR, BUCURESTI
(Autonomous Directorate Of Petroleum And Natural Gas, Bucharest)

Bucharest — Romania, 109, Calea Victoriei, Sector 1, Telephone: 14 71 90; Telex: 11720

Discharges the functions assigned to industrial centrals and departments, providing leadership for all petroleum and gas extraction units.

CENTRALA GAZULUI METAN, MEDIAS
(Methane Gas Central, Medias)

Medias — Romania, 4, Unirii St., Sibiu County, Telephone: 12262; Telex: 49718

Natural Gas prospecting, well drilling, production and transport of natural gas, constructions, installations, laying of pipelines, research, design, service regarding these activities; natural gas burning and control equipment installation and equipment repair for the methane gas industry.

COMBINATUL MINIER, VALEAJIULUI
(Mining Combine, Valea Jiului)

Petrosani — Romania, Hunedoara County, 2, 23 August Street, Telephone: 957/40460

Coal output and processing; geological, mining and industrial construction; production of mechanization equipment and installations for the coal industry, spare parts, metallic structures for the coal industry, repair and workover jobs (mining equipment), research, design, and manufacture of mining equipment.

CENTRALA INEREURILOR, DEVA
(Ores Central, Deva)

Deva — Romania, Deva County, 4, Piata Unirii, Telephone: 956/13640; Telex: 32223

Output of ferrous, non-ferrous and gold-bearing ores and ore concentrates; geological surveys and investigations; mining and industrial constructions, research and design, related services.

CENTRALA MINEREURILOR SI METALURGIEI NEFEROASE, BAIA MARE
(Nonferrous Ores and Metallurgy Central, Baia Mare)

Baia Mare — Romania, Maramures County, Piata Gh. Gheorghiu Dej, Telephone: 994/11504; Telex: 33223

Output of non-ferrous ores and non-ferrous ore concentrates; output of heavy non-ferrous metals and associated metals from concentrates; geological surveys and investigations; mining and industrial constructions; research and design; production and repair of mining equipment.

CENTRALA SARII SI NEMETALIFERELOR, BUCURESTI
(Salt And Non-Metallic Ores Central, Bucharest)

Bucharest — Romania, 220, Calea Victoriei, Sector 1, Telephone: 50 40 78; Telex: 10647

Output of salt from non-metallic ores and concentrates; geological surveys; mining and industrial construction; research and design; related services.

COMBINATUL MINIER, PLOIESTI
(Mining Combine, Ploiesti)

Ploeisti — Romania, Prohova County, 2 Bobilna St., Telephone: 971/23610

Output and cleaning of lignite and brown coal, mine and pit opening; research and manufacture of lignite mining equipment, spare parts and subassemblies, repair of mining and transportation equipment.

COMBINATUL MINIER, OLTENIA
(Mining Combine, Oltenia)

Farcasesti — Romania, Gorj County, Telephone: 929/134

Output and dressing of lignite, research, design and execution of geological, hydrogeological and draining works, mine and pit opening.

Industrial Constructions Ministry

CENTRALA DE MECANIZARE PENTRU CONSTRUCTII INDUSTRIALE, BUCURESTI — C.M.C.I.B.
(Industrial Constructions Mechanization Central, Bucharest)

Bucharest — Romania, 164, Sos Giurgiului, Sector 5, Telephone: 85 34 90; Telex: 11605

Repair of building machinery and equipment; production of building machinery, equipment, devices and tools.

Forest Economy And Building Materials Ministry

CENTRALA DE PRELUCRARE A LEMNULUI, BUCURESTI
(Woodworking Central, Bucharest)

Bucharest — Romania, 46-48 Sos. Pipera, Sector 2, Telephone: 33 55 40; Telex: 11380

Coordinates woodworking complexes and enterprises, timber factories, plywood and veneer factories, particle board factories, furniture and carpentry factories, parquetry and wood container factories.

CENTRALA DE EXPLOATARE A LEMNULUI, BUCURESTI
(Lumbering Central, Bucharest)

Bucharest — Romania, 8, Calomfirescu St., Sector 4, Telephone: 14 52 62; Telex: 11221

Coordinates log output and transport enterprises.

CENTRALA MATERIALELOR DE CONSTRUCTII, BUCURESTI
(Building Materials Central, Bucharest)

Bucharest — Romania, 136, Calea Grivitei, Sector 8, Telephone: 17 53 00; Telex: 10569

Coordinates enterprises producing building materials, bricks, tiles, sandstone and marble plates, sanitary items, prefab concrete panels for constructions, asbestos-cement and cast iron drain pipes, insulation materials for construction, etc.

CENTRALA CIMENTULUI, BUCURESTI
(Cement Central, Bucharest)

Bucharest — Romania, 8, Calomfirescu St., Sector 4, Telephone: 15 09 36; Telex: 10249

Coordinates cement, plaster and lime producing enterprises.

CENTRALA DE UTILAJE SI PIESE DE SCHIMB, BUCURESTI
(Equipment And Spare Parts Central, Bucharest)

Bucharest — Romania, 12, Preciziei Blvd., Sector 7, Telephone: 60 74 30; Telex: 10587

Coordinates enterprises producing equipment and spare parts for units subordinated to the Forest Economy and Building Materials Ministry.

CENTRALA DE CELULOZA, HIRTIE SI FIBRE ARTIFICIALE, BRAILA
(Pulp, Paper and Artificial Fibre Central, Braila)

Braila — Romania, Sos. Braila-Viziru, Km 10, Telephone: 938/31239; Telex: 55219

Coordinates combines and enterprises producing pulp, paper goods and artificial fibres.

DEPARTMENTUL SILVICULTURII
(Forestry Department)

Bucharest — Romania, 21 Calea Grivitei, Sector 4, Telephone: 150680

Coordinates national scale forestry activity; preservation and development of the growing stock: afforestation, improvement of species, phytosanitary campaigns, and marketing of forest by-products (fruit, mushrooms, resin, seeds, fodder, honey, etc.). Protection, industrial-scale development and management of game and salmonidae (trout); environment protection achieved by zoning and management of forests and hydrographic basins, correction, etc.

CENTRALA DE EXPLOATARE INDUSTRIALA A AGREGATELOR MINERALE PENTRU CONSTRUCTII, TIRGOVISTE
(Central For Industrial Exploitation Of Building Mineral Agglomerates, Tirgoviste)

Tirgoviste — Romania, Dimbovita County, Castanilor Blvd., Telephone: 926/12058

Coordinates the work of the building mineral agglomerates.

Agriculture And Food Industry Ministry

CENTRALA INDUSTRIALIZARII CARNII, BUCURESTI
(Meat Industrialization Central, Bucharest)

Bucharest — Romania, 3, Piata Valter Maracineanu, Telephone: 15 91 04; Telex: 10392

Meat and meat products.

CENTRALA INDUSTRIALIZARII LAPTELUI, BUCURESTI
(Milk Industrialization Central, Bucharest)

Bucharest — Romania, 3, Piata Valter Maracineanu, Telephone: 14 43 95; Telex: 11193

Dairy Products.

CENTRALA PRODUCTIEI SI INDUSTRIALIZARII PESTELUI, BUCURESTI
(Fish Breeding And Fish Industrialization Central, Bucharest)

Bucharest — Romania, 3, Piata Valter Maracineanu, Telephone: 14 84 52

Fish and fishery products.

CENTRALA PRODUCTIEI SI INDUSTRIALIZARII SFECLEI DE ZAHAR, BUCURESTI
(Sugar Beet Production And Industrialization Central, Bucharest)

Bucharest — Romania, 3, Piata Valter Maracineanu, Telephone: 13 92 03; Telex: 10056

Sugar.

CENTRALA BERII, SPIRTULUI SI AMIDONULUI, BUCURESTI
(Beer, Alcohol And Starch Central, Bucharest)

Bucharest — Romania, 157 Calea Rahovei, Sector 6, Telephone: 23 81 10; Telex: 10462

Various types of beer, alcohol and starch.

CENTRALA PRODUCTIEI SI INDUSTRIALIZARII TUTUNULUI, BUCURESTI
(Tobacco Production And Industrialization Central, Bucharest)

Bucharest — Romania, 2, Regiei Blvd., Sector 7, Telephone: 49 71 45; Telex: 10696

Tobacco and cigarettes.

CENTRALA ULEIULUI, BUCURESTI
(Oil Central, Bucharest)

Bucharest — Romania, 2, Spataru Preda St., Sector 6, Telephone: 23 70 70; Telex: 10860

Vegetable oil and derivatives.

CENTRALA VALORIFICARII A CEREALELOR SI PRODUCEREA NUTRETURILOR COMBINATE, BUCURESTI
(Central For Marketing Grain And Production Of Compound Fodder, Bucharest)

Bucharest — Romania, 17 Republicii Blvd., Telephone: 14 22 10; Telex: 11611 ABCD

Contracting, purchase, preservation and marketing of grain. Industrial production of compound fodder.

CENTRALA PENTRU LEGUME SI FRUCTE, BUCURESTI
(Fruit And Vegetables Central, Bucharest)

Bucharest — Romania, 2, Dr. Marcovic St., Telephone: 16 28 04; Telex: 10530

Fresh, half-preserved and tinned vegetables and fruit, and potatoes.

CENTRALA VIEI SI VINULUI, BUCURESTI
(Vineyard And Wine Central, Bucharest)

Bucharest — Romania, 2 Dr. Marcovic St., Telephone: 15 39 96; Telex: 11649

Wines and alcoholic drinks.

CENTRALA DE MECANIZAREA AGRICULTURII SI PRODUCEREA DE UTILAJE PENTRU AGRICULTURA SI INDUSTRIA ALIMENTARA, BUCURESTI
(Central For Agriculture Mechanization And Production Of Farming And Food Industry Equipment, Bucharest)

Bucharest — Romania, 24, Republicii Blvd., Sector 4, Telephone: 14 40 20; Telex: 10737

Undertakes the mechanization of agriculture.

TRUSTUL INULUI, CINEPII SI BUMBACULUI
(Flax, Hemp And Cotton Trust)

Bucharest — Romania, 2, Dr. Marcovici St., Telephone: 13 68 80; Telex: 10664

Organization of production, contracting and purchase of flax and hemp straws and cotton. Processing and marketing of flax and hemp straws.

TRUSTUL PLANTELOR MEDICALE "PLAFAR" ("Plafar" Medicinal Herbs Trust)

Bucharest — Romania, 50, Emil Bodnaras St., Telephone: 60 56 55; Telex: 104366

Production, purchase, processing and marketing of medicinal herbs and aromatic plants.

CENTRALA INDUSTRIALA DE MORARIT, DECORTICAT, PANIFICATIE SI PRODUSE FAINOASE
(Industrial Central For Milling, Decortication, Bakery And Flour Products)

Bucharest — Romania, 3, Piata Valter Maracineanu, Telephone: 14 24 13, Telex: 10468

Production of flour, maize flour, bread, flour paste ware and biscuits, rice decortication.

CENTRALA DELTA DUNARII
(Delta Dunarii Central)

Tulcea — Romania, Tulcea County, 1, Piata Republicii, Telephone: 14660; Telex: 52237

Capitalization of the resources of the Danube Delta (fishing, fish breeding, reed cultivation).

Light Industry Ministry

CENTRALA INDUSTRIEI BUMBACULUI, BUCURESTI
(Cotton Industry Central, Bucharest)

Bucharest — Romania, 2, Sos. Morarilor, Sector 3, Telephone: 27 60 80; Telex: 11265

Coordinates the production of: cotton and cotton type yarns and fabrics (bleached or dyed fabrics for bed sheeting, 100 p.c. cotton or mixed cotton and rayon and polyester; fabrics designed for clothing, piece-dyed, yarn-dyed or printed, or cotton or mixed cotton and rayon or polyester; shirtings, piece-dyed, yarn-dyed or printed, of mixed cotton and rayon and polyester; 100 p.c. rayon sateen lustre creaseless printed fabrics for dresses; printed fabrics for dresses of mixed cotton and polyester or rayon; checkered fabrics and flannels for sport shirts; suitings of cotton and mixed cotton and polyester; yarn-dyed cotton pajama fabrics; cotton and mixed cotton and polyester sewing thread; cotton and rayon yarns; technical fabrics).

Cotton and mixed yarns bedding (sheets, pillowcases, bed sets). Various textile raw materials (cotton and mixed yarns).

CENTRALA INDUSTRIEI MATASII, INULUI SI CINEII, BUCURESTI
(Silk, Flax and Hemp Industry Central, Bucharest)

Bucharest — Romania, 134, Ghencea Blvd., Sector 6, Telephone: 31 64 00; Telex: 1183758

Pure silk, artificial silk and synthetic fibre fabrics (printed artificial fibre fabrics — acetate, triacetate or mixed type; plain or printed pure silk fabrics; printed nylon and polyester fabrics; printed pure silk, polyester, acetate or triacetate neckties; pure silk and polyester jacquard neckties; pure silk and artificial silk kerchiefs and scarves). Decorative fabrics (jacquard or schaft pattern upholstery fabrics; decorative artificial silk and mixed jacquard pattern fabrics; cotton or mixed fibre plush for furniture and home decoration; various fabrics blankets; fringes, elastic and non-elastic ribbons and other trimmings; hats, cloche hats, berets and fezzes). Linen and hemp fabrics (for garments and bedding; linen and hemp — in admixture with other fibres — fabrics for table cloths and napkins; indoor decoration fabrics, camping articles; tarpaulins). Various textile raw materials (silk waste, flax and hemp bundle; non-rubberized fire hoses — 100 percent polyester; silk and polyester yarns; mixed flax and polyester yarns).

CENTRALA INDUSTRIEI LINII, BUCURESTI
(Wool Industry Central, Bucharest)

Bucharest — Romania, 300, Sos. Pantelimon, Sector 3, Telephone: 27 44 80; Telex: 11510

Woolen carpets, blankets and cloth (machine-made carpets — 100 percent wool or in admixture with synthetic and artificial fibres; tufting carpets — woolen or in admixture with synthetic or artificial fibres; suitings — 100 percent wool or in admixture with synthetic or artificial fibres; blankets — 100 percent wool or in admixture with synthetic fibres or 100 percent synthetic fibres; cotton and vicuna blankets). Various textile raw materials (technical felt for hydroinsulating support and upholstery requisites); flaw wool for carpets.

CENTRALA INDUSTRIEI TRICOTAJELOR, BUCURESTI
(Knitwear Industry Central, Bucharest)

Bucharest — Romania, 220 Calea Serban Voda, Sector 5, Telephone: 23 68 90; Telex: 11664

Knitwear (cotton knitted underwear — men's undershirts, pants, trunks, pajamas, flannel or plush underwear; cotton knitted outerwear — T-shirts, terrycloth sweatsuits, polo and tennis shirts, sweat shirts, etc.; polyamide yarn garments — ladies' slips, nighties and panties, nylon, helanca — in admixture with cotton — track suits, etc.; acrylic knitwear —pullovers, jackets, slacks, dresses, overcoats, wintercoats, sets of pullovers, sets of jackets and trousers, gloves, caps, berets); cotton, acrylic, helanca or polyamide fibres, socks and stockings for men, women and children; synthetic and artificial yarn tights.

CENTRALA INDUSTRIEI CONFECTIILOR, BUCURESTI
(Garments Industry Central, Bucharest)

Bucharest — Romania, 7, Armata Poporului Blvd., Sector 7, Telephone: 31 00 70; Telex: 11195

Ready-mades for men, women, teenagers and children (indoor and outdoor garments, sport and travel wear, underwear, protection clothes, school uniforms, workmen's special clothes).

CENTRALA INDUSTRIEI PIELARIEI, CAUCIUCULUI SI INCALTAMINTEI, BUCURESTI
(Leatherwear, Rubber And Footwear Industry Central, Bucharest)

Bucharest — Romania, 96, Splaiul Unirii, Sector 5, Telephone: 20 60 20; Telex: 11523, 10154

Leather and artificial leather footwear for men, women and children; leather and leather substitute gloves; protection gloves; morocco goods; fur and leather garments; rubber footwear and sport articles; plastic-made toys and other articles, pvc foils; artificial leather and plastic foils.

CENTRALA INDUSTRIEI STICLARIEI SI CERAMICII FINE, BUCURESTI
(Glass And Fine Ceramics Industry Central, Bucharest)

Bucharest — Romania, 171, Muncii Blvd., Sector 3, Telephone: 27 30 40; Telex: 11869

FOREIGN TRADE ORGANIZATIONS

AGROEXPORT

Bucharest — Romania, 2, Ion Ghica St., Telephone: 13 71 72; Telex: 11141

Exports: Grain; oleaginous seeds, leguminous and technical plants; flour; grain and fodder exchange.

Imports: Grain; oleaginous seeds; leguminous and technical plants; flour; grain and fodder exhange.

ARCOM
(Romanian Construction And Erection Company)

Bucharest — Romania, 91-93, Calea Victoriei, Telephone: 14 98 33; Telex: 11490

Exports: Engineering services, licenses, technology, designs and surveys in the field of construction.

Construction of industrial projects, socio-cultural centers, administrative buildings, hospitals, hotels and housing, as a general contractor or civil engineer, singly or in association with local partners or third parties.

Technical assistance in designing and constructing projects.

Services in the field of construction.

Imports: Purchasing of machinery, installations, devices, transport equipment and materials required on its sites.

ARPIMEX

Bucharest — Romania, 1, Al. Postolache St., Telephone: 31 32 60; Telex: 11472; POB: 5650

Exports: Footwear with leather and leather substitute uppers for men, women and children; leather gloves for men and women; protection gloves; leatherwear (handbags, folios, attache cases, beauty cases, bags, saddlery, etc.); fur and leather garments; pvc foils; vinyl on textile support; pvc carpets; household items; rubber and sport items; rubber footwear; lohn operations.

Imports: Raw sheepskins, goatskins and cowhides; leather; tanning materials; organic dyes and pigments; chemical auxiliaries for the leather industries; other raw materials, auxiliary materials for leather and footwear industry, inclusively for rubber footwear, plastic articles and artificial leather.

AUTO-DACIA

Bucharest — Romania, 19, Lipscani St., Telephone: 15 86 20; Telex: 11396

Exports: Motor cars; four-wheel-drive cars; buses; utility vans; special purpose vehicles derived from motor cars; special purpose vehicles derived from utility vans; CKD and SKD; related spare parts and mounting lines; service.

Imports: Components, subassemblies, CKD and SKD for the manufacture of specific products; spare parts for the specific products; motor cars; four-wheel-drive cars; buses; utility vans; special purpose vehicles derived from motor cars; special purpose vehicles derived from utility vans.

AUTOEXPORTIMPORT

2200 — Brasov — Romania, 45, Republicii St., Telephone: 921 40 133; Telex: 12268, 12269

Exports: Trucks of 3-30 tons with 2, 4 and 6 drive wheels, tractors, dump trucks, special purpose vehicles, trailers; assembly lines.

Imports: Trucks, dump trucks, special purpose vehicles, tractors, and electric, hydraulic and pneumatic equipment for motor vehicle production.

CHIMIMPORTEXPORT

Bucharest — Romania, 10, Republicii Blvd., Telephone: 16 06 36; Telex: 11184, 11185; POB: 525

Exports: Inorganic substances; intermediaries and organic solvents; alkylamines; organic acids; synthetic and plastic resins; synthetic rubber of the butadiene-styrene type — CAROM® trademark; carbon black; pest-fighters; organo-phosphoric insecticides; pharmaceutical raw materials; original pharmaceutical preparations; conditioned medical drugs; organic pigments and dyestuffs; intermediaries for dyestuffs production; inks and lacquers; thinners; inorganic pigments; plasticizers; soaps and detergent granules; perfumery products and cosmetics; chemical reagents.

Imports: Natural and synthetic rubber, polyethylene, polypropylene, colophony, sulfur, chromium ore, ammonium chloride, fatty alcohols, chlorine hydride, polystyrene, cellophane, reagents, adhesives, catalysts and other chemicals which are not included in the export lists of other foreign trade companies; medical drugs (veterinary drugs excluded), raw materials for cosmetics, dyestuffs (those used in the light industry are excluded), intermediaries, pharmaceuticals, boron ore, naphthalene, organic solvents, styrene, titanium dioxide, zinc oxide, glycerine, plasticizers, bone and hide glue, suet, vegetable oils (tung oil, linseed oil and coconut oil) lacquers and dyes, melamine, organic and inorganic pigments, stearine soaps, etc.

COMTURIST

Bucharest — Romania, 40-44, 30 Decembrie St., Telephone: 15 05 97; 13 59 89; Telex: 1117; POB: 833

Company selling goods at home with payment in freely convertible currency.

Comturist shops are to be found in Bucharest, Brasov and in the Black Sea coast resorts.

Goods can be bought either directly from the usual shops with payment in cash or from Special Order Shops where payment is made in checks, payment orders, letters of credit.

Comturist Agency offers: Romanian automobiles; long-term technical goods (refrigerators, heating stoves, washing machines, etc.); carpets, furniture; various other goods (handicrafts, fur and leather coats, cosmetics, cigarettes, drinks, etc.); automotive spare parts.

CONFEX

Bucharest — Romania, 7, Armata Poporului Blvd., Telephone: 31 37 51; Telex: 11195 c conf-r

Exports: All types of ladies' wear, men's wear, teenagers' wear and children's wear; everyday dress; sports dress, traveling dress; formal dress; house dress; knitwear dress.

CONTRANSIMEX

Bucharest — Romania, 38, Dinicu Golescu Blvd., Telephone: 18 00 42, Telex: CTRIX 11606, A, B; POB: 2006

Exports: Studies, projects, documentation, licenses, technical assistance, services, expert's accounts and carrying out of erection-mounting jobs and installations in the fields of transports and telecommunications abroad (highways, motorways, railways, level crossings, tunnels, channels, bridges, ports, airports, telecommunication jobs); box-pallets and containers and other products produced by transport and telecommunication units.

Imports: Complex installations and technological completion equipment for the projects of the Transport and Telecommunications Ministry, licenses, technical documentation and assistance included; machinery, installations and working devices for building and repair jobs in the fields of rail, road and water transport, traffic signaling and security; electrification of railway jobs (which are not carried out by other foreign trade companies); ship repairs; garage equipment; mail and telecommunications machines and equipment which are not imported by other foreign trade companies; portal and semi-portal, floating and railway cranes; spare parts for maintenance and repair jobs in the field of rail, road and water transport, mail and telecommunications (spare parts for Dacia motor cars excepted); pit coal creosote; fishing tools for industrial fishing jobs; equipment and materials for assembling jobs carried out abroad.

DANUBIANA

Bucharest — Romania, 202 A, Splaiul Independentei, Telephone: 49 50 10; 49 50 60; Telex: 11489 danaz r; 11748 danzar r; 11842 danzar r; POB: 2350

Exports: Chemical fertilizers, urea, ammonium nitrate, calcium ammonium nitrate, complex fertilizers, diammonium phosphate, superphosphate; radial and conventional tires as well as inner tubes for passenger cars, trucks, tractors, industrial and agricultural vehicles; technical rubber items; reclaimed rubber, V-belts, conveyor belts, high and low pressure tubes and hoses, accumulator hard rubber cases, profiled and pressed rubber gaskets, rubber car carpets; processed plastic items; PVC granules, foils, sheetings, floorings, pipes, tubes, profiles, simple and corrugated plates; polyethylene blown films, sacks and bags, injection molded articles for industry or consumer goods (barrels, cans, baskets etc.), thermoformed polystyrene products; chemical fibres and yarns; polyacryl, polyamide, polypropylene, polyester; adipic acid, cellulosic film; other chemical items; sodium nitrate, ammonium bicarbonate, butanol, methyl acetate, butyl acetate, etc.

Imports: Phosphates; sulfuric acid; phosphoric acid; ion exchangers; catalysts; arsenic anhydride; monoethanolamine; diethanolamine; divinylbenzene; synthetic camphor; sodium sulphite; sodium sulfate; morpholine; photo gelatine; tires; anti-oxidant; antiozone; accelerators for vulcanization (Vulcacite); cord net; rubber and plastic technical and insulation products (all assortments); chemical pulp; chemicals for the chemical fibres and yarns production.

DELTA

Bucharest — Romania, 2, Intrarea Bibliotecii, Telephone: 15 00 71; Telex: 10570 Delta R; POB: 796; Cables: DELTA — Bucharest

Exports: Chemical and petrochemical products, wood, wooden products, metal products, building materials, household articles, barter operations, triangular operations, etc.

Imports: Various goods.

ELECTROEXPORTIMPORT

Bucharest — Romania, 133, Calea Victoriei, Telephone: 50 28 70; Telex: 11388; POB: 17

Exports: Electric motors; electric generators, welding converters powered by electric motors or heat engines; power capacitors; electrical insulation materials; galvanic cells and batteries; electric cables and conductors; lifts; household electric consumer goods (refrigerators, vacuum cleaners, washing machines); indoor and outdoor lighting fixtures, power and distribution transformers, high voltage equipment (switches, separators, lightning arresters, current and voltage transformers); electrical handtools, accumulators; diesel electric and electric locomotives, elevators.

Imports: Rotary electric machines; electric motors; high voltage transformers and apparatus and electrical engineering equipment; carbon brushes for electric machines, equipment for the electric cable and conductor industry, winding benches; electric handtools; household electric consumer goods (refrigerators, sewing machines, washing machines); electrical insulation materials, insulators, accumulators; electric welding equipment; electric cables and conductors, accessories; electric locomotives and streetcars; electric furnaces (excepting those designed for steel and iron alloy production); licenses, invention patents, surveys, designs, know-how, engineering, technical assistance in the field of the electric engineering industry.

ELECTRONUM

Bucharest — Romania, 8, Dimitrie Pompei Blvd., Telephone: 33 71 70; Telex: 11547, 11584; POB: 105

Exports: Computing Technique — medium and small capacity electronic computing systems; minicomputers, microcomputers; industrial process monitoring computing systems; off-line equipment for computing systems; integrated circuits invoicing and accounting machines; desk-top electronic computers (with display or printer); pocket electronic computers; electro-mechanical computing machines (two or three operations).

Black and White TV Sets — fixed TV sets with 47,51,59,61,65 cm. kinescope hybrid or with printed circuits (modular system); portable television sets of 31 cm. kinescope, fully transistorized or with printed circuits (modular system).

Radio Receivers — MA-MF stationary radio receivers; MA-MF portable radio receivers; 3 band MA radio receivers for motor cars; TV-OIRT, RETMA, CCIR-VHF selectors; television and radio parts and components.

Passive Electronic Components — ceramic capacitors; semi-variable capacitors-trimmers; by-pass capacitors; resistors; varistors; thermistors; passive networks, resistors, capacitors.

Kinescopes of 44,47,51,59,61 and 65 cm.

Electronic Guns, TE1 and TE2.

Active Electronic Components — integrated circuits-linear and logical; silicon transistors; germanium transistors; silicon diodes; germanium diodes; thyristors; power rectifying diodes; radiators; rectifying bridges.

Ferrites — complete set of ferrite cores for the television deflection system; anisotrope magnets for loudspeakers; magnetic tape for refrigerators; aerials for radio receivers; magnetic segments for electric motors; transmission paths; E-type transformer cores; plasto-ferrite rectification and focusing magnets; sets of radio-shielding plugs for motor cars.

Connectors — linear connectors for double-plated printed circuits; linear plug-in connectors for automated telephone exchanges and carrier currents; rotary plug-in connectors with seven contacts 6+ mass); RACK plug-in connectors with 9,15,25,37,50 contacts; switches for television sets and radio receivers; parts and accessories for the electronic industry (line straight boxes, jacks, sockets, etc.).

Electric Measuring Instruments — measuring bridges with one and six channels; switching-balancing devices; electronic counters; universal and laboratory oscilloscopes; digital and electronic multimeters; versatesters; oscilloscopes-miniscopes; stabilized and continuous voltage source.

Radiotelephones — portable, stationary and mobile radiotelephones.

Electric Measuring Instruments — double tariff and CAM-63 single-phase counters; CA43 S, CA32 S three-phase and double tariff counters; MI, AI indicating milliamperemeters; LI indicatinglogometers; wattmeters, varimeters; electromagnetic and magnetoelectric apparatus.

Electric Installation Equipment — current breakers; switches, plugs; sockets; high breaking capacity and standard fuses; industrial sockets and plug-ins.

Low Voltage Equipment — automatic circuit breakers, standard and explosion-proof design; contactors, thermal relays; micro circuit breakers, standard and explosion-proof design; push buttons; signaling lamps; cam controllers.

Telephone Exchanges — local, long-distance, tandem, rural, office and hotel telephone exchanges; line concentrators.

Telephone Sets — calling-dial telephone sets; secretary telephone exchanges; flame-proof design mining telephone sets.

Electrical Engineering Automation Equipment — single and three-phase thyristor-equipped static converters; thyristor-equipped speed variators; battery chargers with automatic voltage stabilization for buffer system; rectifiers for electrolytic installations; high voltage electric equipment batteries of condensers for the improvement of the power factor; static excitation equipment for synchronous generators.

Low Voltage Transformers and Autotransformers of Powers Up To 100 KVA — autotransformers; bell transformers; single-phase and three-phase transformers.

Automation Elements — electronic automation instruments: transducers for pressure, temperature, output, water quality, conductivity, pH; indicators; recorders; continuous and discrete regulators; signal converters; analog computing elements; panel secondary elements — auxiliary apparatus; static commutation equipment; fire detecting equipment; photoelectric relays for the automated control of public lighting; electronic time relays. Pneumatic automation instruments (panel mounted or processmounted): — pen and selector recorders; indicating regulators; indicators; integrators; computing elements; function generators; programmers; deviation indicting controllers; local indicating regulators with measuring elements.

Automation Equipment and Installations — distribution and control switchboard; monitoring switchboard; distribution and control panels; distribution and control cabinets; control desks; control boxes; automation relays for use in the industrial, transport and power field.

Reseach and Design in the Field of Industrial Process Automation — research and production of automation equipment and elements; designing of automation systems and installations for all industrial branches; designing of computer-assisted automated process lines and elaboration of basic software; technical assistance and consulting in the commissioning of automation equipment for various industrial processes.

Lighting Sources — standard and special electric bulbs of 25-100 W; fluorescent tubes; mercury vapor lamps with magnesium germanate and with yttrium vanadite; sodium vapor lamps; ballasts, cast-in and cast-off design, for fluorescent tues; ballasts, cast-in and cast-off design, for mercury vapor lamps; allasts for sodium vapor lamps; igniters for sodium vapor lamps.

Imports: — Complex installations for the electronic and electrical engineering industry, licenses, patents, studies, knowhow, engineering, technial assistance; computing technique machinery and equipment; typewriters; passive electronic components (resistors, potentiometers, thermistors, fixed and variable capacitors); materials for radio and television set production; active electronic components (semi-conductors, diodes, transistors, thyristors, etc.; electronic valves: reception, emission, picture, special); lighting sources, TV mobile units, various studio electro-acoustic equipment, telecommunication elements; designing of automation systems and installations for all industrial branches; designing of computer-assisted automated process lines and elaboration of basic software; technical assistance and consulting in the commissioning of the automation equipment for various projects.

EXIMCOOP
(Foreign Trade Department of the Consumer Cooperatives)

Bucharest — Romania 31, Brrezoianu St. Telephone: 13 64 33;
Telex: 11591 a-b

Exports: — Edible egg paste, egg powder, industrial egg powder, feathers, human hair, snails, frogs, frogs' legs, pigeons, rabbits, bees' honey and wax, beans and pumpkin seeds.

Imports: — Products designed to meet the needs of cooperatives (CENTROCOOP) which are not covered by other foreign trade companies.

FOREXIM

Bucharest — Romania 6, Edgar Quinet St. Telephone: 16 11 33;
Telex: 11120

Exports: — Licenses, surveys, technical documentation and projects worked out by own staff of the ministry institutes, engineering technical assistance, spare parts and cooperation ventures regarding installations for silviculture, the wood-processing industry, the pulp and paper industry, the building materials industry; equipment and spare parts turned out by the forest economy and building material units.

Imports: — Factories, complex installations, technological installations, subassemblies, documentation, projects, technical assistance and spare parts for the wood processing industry, the pulp and paper industry, the building materials industry (cement factories excluded); tools, cutters and devices for wood procesing, pulp, paper and building materials processing, phosphorous bronze sieves; licenses, surveys, technical documentation, projects, know-how, technical assistance for factories, complex installations, technological completion installations and spare parts for the wood processing industry, the pulp and paper, and building materials (cement factories excluded) industries.

FRUCTEXPORT

Bucharest — Romania 43, Brezoianu St. Telephone: — 13 65 63;
Telex: 10963; Cables: Fructexport — Bucharest

Exports: — Fresh orchard and hothouse fruit for household use; fresh orchard and forest fruit for industrial use; fresh hothouse and field vegetables for household use; grown and wild mushrooms: fresh, dried and in rine; semi-industrialized products: pulps, purees, juices, concentrated apple juice; dehydrated fruit and vegetables; walnuts in shell walnut kernels; canned fruit: — in waer, in light and heavy syrup, james, purees, nectars, syrups; canned vegetables in water, in vinegar, in oil or in tomato sauce; tomato paste and juice; frozen fruit and vegetables for household and industrial use; flowers and ornamental plants; medicinal plants, seeds and essential oils.

GEOMIN
(Company For Mining And Geological Cooperation)

Bucharest — Romania
109, Calea Victoriei
Telephone: 14 55 01; Telex: 11242

Carries out geological investigations, preliminary evaluations, laboratory analyses, technological research, feasibility studies, surveys, designs, construction-erection jobs, mining and geological engineering jobs; complete installation plants for mining projects, turnkey deliveries or ore processing plants; participation in joint mining ventures abroad.

Imports: — Installations and equipment for mining ore processing projects under construction abroad.

ICECOOP

Bucharest — Romania
12, Marin Serghiescu St.
Telephone: — 12 10 69; Telex: 10 479

Exports: — Furniture, wooden articles (toys for little children, household items, handicrafts), wrought iron and copper. Oriental-type hand-knotted carpets. Kelim-type hand-woven carpets, textile handicrafts (fabrics, folk embroideries, folk garments, blouses and dolls), ready-mades and knitwear, black and colored ceramics, basket-work, handicraft glassware, silverware, Christmas tree decorations, leatherwear (footwear, morocco goods, furrier's goods), metallic articles and chemicals, painted wood and glass icons, etc.: — operations: — mainly in the field of ready-mades, footwear and precious metals; services: including selling of products against payment in foreign currency in the trading network of the handicraft cooperatives; goods exchange: — with similar foreign enterprises, organizations and companies; cooperation: — cooperation in the field of goods production and sale in foreign markets.

ILEXIM

Bucharest — Romania
3, 13 Decembrie St.
Telephone: — 15 76 72; Telex: — 11226

Exports: — Wooden and metal household articles; inner decoration articles from wood, metal, glass, alabaster, ceramics; white and decorative candles; handtools and gardening implements; vrious osier, reed, maize leaves and hazel twigs basket-work; occasional furniture with pleated seats; rubber and plastic articles; metallic structures; pig-iron cast articles; various quarry and building materials; certain textile ready-mades; sport and camping outfits; travel and beach articles; school and office requisites; wind and percussion instruments; certain agricultural produce and foodstuffs; table andmedicinal mineral water; books, newspapers, magazines, periodicals, postage stamps and accessories; records.

Imports: — Books, newspapers, magazines, periodicals, postage stamps and accessories; records.

IMPEXMIN

Bucharest Romania
109, Calea Victoriei
Telephone: 50 31 90; Telex: 10588; POB: 4664

Exports: — Raw materials: emulsifying reduction agents, anionic surface active substances, ground asbestos, bentonite, organic colloids, kaolin clays, chalk, organofilic clay, dacite, diatomite, dolomite, bleaching earths, emulsifying agents for drilling fluids, feldspar, kaolin, quartz, quartz mass, filter agents, rock salt, quartz sand for foundries, mineral specimens, talc, witherite. Processed products: — tools and apparatus used in oil and gas drilling (fishing too magnets, dynamographs, weight indicators, multiple shot survey instruments for recording the direction and inclination of bore holes, torque assembly, pressure recorders, etc.); devices for pipes (safety devices, natural gas pressure adjusting installations, industrial pressure regulators, gas filters for regulating stations, tronsons rotary devices, burners with radiant flame type TRICEM, burners in group); mining equipment and products for dressing (fixed trucks, hydrocyclones, electric sludge pumps, mechanical agitators, sample takers); diverse goods (rubber pistons, various rubber gaskets, rubber protectors, drillpipe wipers, miners' helmets).

Imports: — Products, equipment and installations for mining, oil and gas industries: — kaolin, kieselguhr, perlite, atapulgite, mica, chalk, steatite, manganese dioxide, hard grinding materials, flotation reagents, ground silica, copper, lead and zinc concentrates, steam coal, preparation plants for non-metal-bearing ores, complete technological lines, mechanized systems for coal face cutters, winches and extraction machines, loading machines for bags, drill carriages (JUMBO), perforating heads, geologic drilling installations, pumps for the mining industry, compressors, ventilators, pit lamps, apparatus for mine rescue, transformer substations of fire-proof design, fire-proof electric apparatus, equipment, apparatus and materials for offshore platforms, spare parts for mining and oil equipment, pumps and valves, etc. Gas processing plants, equipment for cryogenic plants, etc.

INDUSTRIALEXPORT

Bucharest — Romania
1-3, Scaune St.
Telephone: 13 10 09; Telex: 10052; POB: 768

Exports: — Complete oil refineries and complex chemical and petrochemical installations, parts of installations and technological lines in the field of chemical and petrochemical industries and of crude processing; drilling rigs and equipment, production equipment for crude and gas wells, geological investigation and water well drilling equipment, mining equipment, pumps and industrial fittings; studies, designs, technical assistance in construction jobs, training of operating personnel and other engineering jobs and services in the field of oil equipment, oil refineries, chemical and petrochemical units.

Imports: — Completion outfits for complex chemical and oil processing installations and equipment specific to oil and gas extraction industry; industrial fittings; pumps.

Cooperates with specialist firms in other countries in building industrial units, development of technologies in the cheical industry and crude processing, as well as in the manufacture of oil exploration and mining equipment.

MASINEXPORTIMPORT

Bucharest — Romania
1-3, Scaune St.
Telephone: 13 75 96; 33 27 20; Telex: 11206, 11216
Cables: MEXIM — Bucharest

Exports: — Metal cutting machine tools; engine lathes in the range of 400 to 800 mm swing and 750 to 5000 mm length; single spindle automatic lathes 16-25-42-60 mm; turret lathes 32-40-63-80 mm; vertical boring mills with maximum processing diameters of 1400-1650-2200-3300 and 4300 mm; horizontal boring mills, 85-100-130 and 150 mm spindle diameter; plane milling machines, 660-1000 and 1600 mm table width; knee type milling machines (universal and ertical); spur gear hobbing machines; toolroom milling machines; broaching machines; cylindrical grinding machines; surface grinding machines; centerless grinding machines; tool and cutter grinding machines; bench and column drilling machines; vertical inner tapping machines; shaping machines, 425-700 and 800 mm stroke; metal cutting circular and hack saws; ball flashing and lapping machines; ball bearing race lapping machines; hydraulic press brakes; inclinable automatic presses; roll plate bending machines; flanging machines; structural steel shears; profile and section shears; guillotine shears; forging hammers; double-end grinders. Woodworking machines. Textile industry machines. Measuring instruments (mass, length, pressure). Tools.

Imports: — MASINEXPORTIMPORT is sole importer of machine tools in Romania.

MECANOEXPORTIMPORT

Bucharest — Romania
10, Mihai Eminescu St.
Telephone: 12 46 00; Telex: 10269; POB: 130

Exports: — Freight cars and passenger railway cars, tank cars, spare parts, assembly lines for the above mentioned items, relevant components and subassemblies; building equipment roadbuilding equipment, crushing and screening equipment; mechanical handling equipment, electric lift trucks and sideloaders, metallic construction, cast and forged parts; Diesel hydraulic, Diesel electric locomotives and mining locomotives, 4HP-30HP and 120 HP Diesel engines; stationary gasoline engines, compressors; technological equipment for secondary thermal treatment, foundry furnaces and installations included: cast iron and brass sanitary fittings.

Imports: — Mechanical handling equipment (portal and semiportal cranes, floating cranes and railway cranes excluded), motor and electric lift trucks, motor and electric sideloaders; freight cars and passenger railway cars, tank cars; excavators building equipment (excepting road building and railway building equipment); furnaces and technological equipment for foundries, gas-heated secondary thermal treatment furnaces; pressure casting machines (for ferrous and nonferrous metals); asbestos sheets, railway car connections, industrial filters and filtering equipment; compressors, blowers and fans for commercial refrigeration installations and the food industry (excepting methane gas turbocompressors in the chemical industry and technological turbo-compressors and turbo-blowers for furnace and coke gas); firefighting equipment, burners and hot air generators, (air conditioning installations for computing centers included), crushing and screening equipment; welding and oxyacetylene output stations; food industry equipment, bottling and packing equipment; stationary internal combustion engines and 3006000 HP Diesel engines (excepting engines imported as spare parts for vehicles); general purpose equipment.

MERCUR

Bucharest — Romania
118, Calea Victoriei
Telephone: 15 66 00; Telex: 11366

Exchange of consumer goods with similar foreign organiations and firms, exchange of goods of the cooperative units with similar foreign organizations; exchange of commercial equipment and furniture, imports of goods on consignment to supply the domestic market stores; imports of foods; imports of cosmetics, metal haberdashery, buttons, costume jewelry, enameled dishes, household glassware, chinaware, pottery, crystals, cutlery, watches, petromax lamps and brackets, ironmongery, hunting arms, sport arms, precious stones, ropes of beads, statuettes, Christmas tree decorations, record players and spare parts, sports and beach articles, toys, smokers' outfits, school and office stationery, musical articles, razor blades; organization of sales of otor car spare parts, motor cars and other longuse goods, home-built, imported or imported on consignment and paid for in foreign currency; shipping abroad of goods purchased by tourists; export of foodstuffs, craftware, guides and propaganda materials marketable in Romanian restaurants opened abroad, at congresses, gastronomic gatherings, exhibition, stands, etc.; import of amusement equipment, spare parts and similar products marketable in restaurants.

Tarom Airlines

Constante Harbor

METALIMPORTEXPORT

Bucharest — Romania
21-25, Mendeleev St.
Telephone: 62 06 21; Telex: 11515 a, b, c;
Cables: Metalimportexport

Exports-Imports: — Steel semifabs, commercial quality and alloy steel bars and profiles, flat products, tubes, drawn wire, pull ropes, nails, welding electrodes, aluminum ingots and aluminum products, other non-ferrous metals ingots and rolled goods.

METAROM

Bucharest — Romania
21-25, Mendeleev St.
Telephone: 15 05 43; Telex: 11705

Exports: — Technologies, licenses, projects, technical assistance in the field of metalworking.

Imports: — Complex installations and completion equipment; machinery, equipment for the ironworking and metalworking industries and for the coke-chemical, refractory products, abrasive and carbon materials industries which are not included in the import lists of other foreign trade specialist companies; turbo-blowers, electric blowers, turbo-compressors and electric compressors for top gas and coke gas (oxygen installations included); electric furnaces for steel and iron alloys smelting, spectro chemical analysis apparatus for assessment of hydrogen, nitrogen, oxygen and other elements in steel; steel and iron alloys smelting, spectrochemical licenses surveys, designs, technology, engineering, know-how, technical assistance for the iron and metal-working industry, for the coke-chemical, the refractory, abrasive and carbon materials industries.

MINERALIMPORTEXPORT

Bucharest — Romania
16, Republicii Blvd.
Telephone: 13 91 67; Telex: 11873 a, b, c

Exports: — Coal tar, Soderberg paste.

Imports: — Iron ore, manganese ore, pyrite, calcined alumina, bauxite, potassium chloride, potassium fertilizers, graphite electrodes, magnesite and chromemagnesite bricks, silica-alumina bricks, silica bricks, silimanite bricks, Corhart bricks and other refractory materials for the glass industry, magnesite and chrome magnesite mortar, furnace coke, foundry coke, coke breeze, aluminum oxide, abrasives, anthracite, coking coal, sinter and caustic magnesite, rutile, calcium fluoride, zirconium, refractory clay, aluminum fluoride, synthetic cyrolite, pitch tar, carbon and cathode blocks, other materials (putties, refractories, foundry fluxes).

NAVLOMAR

Bucharest — Romania
26, Corneliei St.
Telephone: 23 96 00; 31 79 72; Telex: 11781, 11783 a, b, c, d;
POB: 1302

Chartering, shipping agency, ship chandler services; sale of goods and services payable in currency for foreign ships in Romanian ports.

PETROLEXPORT

Bucharest — Romania
139, Calea Plevnei
Telephone: 49 23 32; Telex: 11519 petex r

Exports: — Gasolines; various lube oils; gas oil; fuel oil; paraffins; petroleum asphalt; petroleum coke.

Imports: — Crude oil; special mineral oils; silicon oils; special greases; additives.

PRODEXPORT

Bucharest — Romania
5-9, Gabriel Peri St.
Telephone: 16 16 60; Telex: 11527

Exports: — Live animals (cattle, sheep, porcines), meat, tinned meat and meat products, Sibiu salami, animal organs and byproducts, frozen poultry, eggs, sugar, sunflower oil, sturgeon, zander fillet, ocean fish, canned fish, caviar, crayfish tails — frozen and in brine, crayfish soup, frogs' legs, live and shot game, bees honey and apiarian products, dairy products, tobacco, cigarettes, etc.

Imports: — Cocoa beans, hop, malt, tobacco, auxiliaries for the foodstuffs industry, etc.

ROMAGRIMEX

Bucharest — Romania
16 Alexandru Sahia St.

Telephone: 14 10 88; 13 48 29; Telex: 11522, 11693
Cables: ROMEX-R

Exports: — Surveys, projects, licenses, technical documentation, know-how, technical assistance in the field of land management and marketing of arable areas, land reclamation, dams and river improvement projects; general supplier of complete installations; equipment and installations included in the manufacturing program of the units subordinated to the Agriculture and Food Industry Ministry, immersion evaporators, cold accumulatos and open basins; smooth pipe cooling elements; air coolers of large capacity (between 110-550 sq.m apiece); heat exchangers; CEF 180 and CEF 250 forced evaporation condensers; forced ventilation water cooling towers (between 50,000 and 600,000 kcal/h for industrial areas — 85 CZ); valves and auxiliary parts for pipes; safety and control fittings; expanded polystyrene shells; equipment for ice factories after the conventional method, excepting compressors, electric pumps, tanks and ice molds; water well drilling, seeds and saplings, breeding and pedigree animals and fowl, in-breeding strains; veterinary medical drugs and products, cooperative ventures, joint production companies sited in Romania or abroad and other forms of cooperation.

Imports: — Protein meal, biostimulators, inseminated eggs; breeding and pedigree animals and fowl, and inbreedin strains, seeds and saplings; biological material for production of sera and vaccines for breeding and zoological purposes; veterinary medical drugs and substances; land reclamation installations and equipment which are not included in the import lists of other importing companies; equipment, installations spare parts and accessories for pre-industrialization of hemp, flax and cotton.

ROMANIAN FILM

Bucharest — Romania
25, Iulius Fucik St.
Telephone: 11 13 08; Telex: 11144

Exports: — Films and tapes for cinematography and television.

Imports: — Films and tapes for cinematography.

ROMANIAN RADIO AND TELEVISION
(Export And Import Board)

Bucharest — Romania
191, Calea Dorobanti
Telephone: 31 15 77; Telex: 11251, 11252, 11746; POB: 111

Exports: — TV films and tapes.

Imports: — TV films and tapes; exchange of TV films

ROMANOEXPORT

Bucharest — Romania
17-19, Doamnei St.
Telephone: 13 36 99, 16 23 10; Telex: 11186, 11400 REXPT R
POB: — 594; Cables: Romanoexport

Exports: — Bleached or dyed bedsheeting, 100 p.c. cotton, cotton mixed with 33 p.c. rayon, various colors; body linen fabrics, piece-dyed, yarn-dyed or printed, of cotton, cotton with 33 p.c. rayon, polyester mixed with cotton or rayon in various designs and colors; shirtings and blouse fabrics, piece-dyed, yarn-dyed or printed, or cotton mixed with 33 p.c. rayon, polyester mixed with cotton, polyester and rayon blends in up-to-date designs and colors; printed fabrics for ladies' dresses of 100 p.c. rayon, sateen lustre, low creasing, in a wide range of designs and colors; printed fabrics for dresses, of polyester mixed with cotton, polyester with rayon, in up-to-date designs and colors; fabrics for sport shirts, checks, checkered flannels, in various designs and colors; suitings of cotton or mixed polyester and cotton, in various weaving effects; cotton pajama fabrics, yarn-dyed, in various designs and colors; various types of sewing thread of cotton or polyester mixed with cotton, in various colors; cotton and rayon yarns; technical cloths; machine-made carpets of 100 p.c. wool and wool mixed with synthetic and artificial fibres; tufted carpets made of wool mixed with artificial and synthetic fibres; piece goods for men's suiting, 100 p.c. wool, wool mixed with synthetic and artificial fibres; blankets, 100 p.c. wool, wool mixed with synthetic fibres, or 100 p.c. synthetic fibres; blankets of cotton and waste cotton; printed fabrics of artificial fibres (acetate, triacetate and mixed fibres); natural silk fabrics, plain, and printed nylon and polyester printed fabrics; printed neckties of natural silk, polyester, acetate and triacetate for men and women; jacquard neckties of natural silk and polyester; scarves and kerchiefs of natural or artificial silk; upholstery fabrics, shaft and jacquard designs, various assortments; decorative jacquard fabrics of artificial silk and mixed fibres; velvets of cotton or cotton mixed with other fibres for upholstery and inner decorations; bedspreads of various fabrics; fringes, elastic ribbons, non-elastic ribbons and other haberdashery; hats and hat bodies; berets and fezzes; linen and hemp fabrics for garments and bedsheetings; linen and hemp and mixed fibres fabrics for table cloths, tables sets and kitchen napkins; linen and hemp fabrics for inner decorations and camping articles; tarpaulins; waste silk; felts and technical cloths; unwoven textiles for hydroinsulation support, upholstery wadding; hemp, bundle, hemp and flax tow, flax and hemp waste fire hose, 100 p.c. polyester, nonrubberized; natural silk and PNA yarns, goat hair; scoured carding carpet wool; yarns: 100 p.c.

cotton and blends; flax yarns blended with polyester; jute scrap bagging rags; mixed new cotton and staple fibre hosiery cuttings; old textile waste; cotton knitted underwear (men's undershirts, men's singlets, trunks, pajamas, plain, dyed and printed, flannels, and terry trousers, interlock and plush); cotton knitted garments (tee-shirts, terry cloth sweatpants and shorts, track suits, polo shirts, sweat shirts); polyamide knitted underwear (ladies' underdresses, nighties, nylon panties, polyester shirts); polyamide knitted garments (track suits of nylon, helanca and cotton); acrylic knitted garments (pullovers, jackets, trousers, dresses, overcoats, sets of pullovers, jackets and trousers, gloves, knitted gloves, caps, mufflers); ladies', children's and men's socks of cotton and acrylic fires, of helanca and polyamide yarns of cotton and rayon and nylon stockings; tights.

Imports: — Raw cotton; carded cotton yarns; woolen waste; jute tow; sisal yarns and fibres; uncoated elastic yarns; ramie; fabrics from plain and teflon-coated glass yarns; glass fibre felting; coated elastic yarns; technical felt, technical cloth for the paper and asbestos cement industries; jute yarns and fabrics; jute and synthetic bags; technical screen for textile printing, for milling and for screen printing; raffia; animal hair; window glass and mirror polishing wheels; textile conveyor belts; spun rayon fibres; wooltype, cottontype, polynosic fibres; acetate, triacetate, viscose and cotton waste yarns; synthetic, polyamide, polyester yarns; metallic and metallized (metallo-plastic) yarns; filter fabrics; synthetic, acrylic fibres for artificial furs; chemical fibres for artificial leather; cotton, wool, silk and blended fabrics; towels; machine-made woolen carpets; polyester jersey; various haberdashery; dye-stuffs; adhesive for interlinings; auxiliaries for the textile and leather industries; pigments for the glassware, pottery and porcelain industries, and bright gold; various chemicals.

ROMCHIM

Bucharest Romania
13, Dacia Blvd.
Telephone: 11 07 30/108; 114; 186; Telex: 10930

Imports: — Complex installations and technological projects, licenses, technological processes, documentation, reproduction rights, technical assistance, services for the chemical and crude processing industries; complex installations and completion equipment for the chemical yarn and fibre industry; industrial fixtures and assembling materials (fittings, flanges) for corrosive chemical media; compressors, blowers and fans for chemical industry technological processes (air, methane gas, commercial refrigeration plants and food industry excepted); pumps for corrosive chemical media; plastic processing equipment; oxygen, nitrogen etc., factories and plants, stocking and distribution stations.

ROMCONSULT
(Romanian Consulting Institute)

Bucharest — Romania
35, Armeneasca St.
Telephone: 12 89 40; Telex: 11650; POB: 757

Carries out a wide range of consulting services; preliminary and feasibility studies; general and execution designs; technical assistance; working out of specifications and organization of tenders; analysis of designs and of other documentation; works supervision; training of personnel; market survey and research; exports of patents, licenses, know-how; managment. The relevant services are carried out in the following spheres: — civil engineering, architecture, town planning, energetics; industry; transports; water supplies; farming; irrigation; education; hydrology, meteorology; tourism; sport.

ROMENERGO

Bucharest — Romania
1, Lacul Tei Blvd.
Telephone: 12 13 26, 12 05 51; Telex: 11525, ROMENG-R
POB: 736

Exports: — High, medium, and low voltage lines, transformer substations and posts, poles and fittings for high, medium and low voltage lines; studies, designs, erection and assembling of projects carried out abroad in the elctric power field, dams, hydrotechnical constructions, export and transport of electric power; licenses, studies, designs, engineering, technical assistance, expert's accounts in the power field.

Imports: — Complex power installations for the electric and nuclear power field, equipment, apparatus and materials for the erection-assembling jobs carried out abroad.

ROMPETROL
(Company For Oil And Gas Cooperation)

Bucharest — Romania
109, Calea Victoriei
Telephone: 14 17 16; Telex: 10155

Carries out abroad: — geological investigations, design, surveys, engineering, and technical assistance in the field of petroleum and gas extraction; oil well drilling jobs, construction of oilfields, petroleum pipelines, oil and natural gas bulk plants and distribution facilities as well as other construction-erection works in the oil and gas industry; participation in joint ventures for hydrocarbon development and production activities; leasing operations.

ROMSIT

Bucharest — Romania
13, Ion Ghica St.
Telephone: 13 89 77, 14 05 32; Telex: 11836, 11855

Exports: — Engineering, consulting complete plants, machinery and aggregates for the light industry sectors household items of metal glass, porcelain, faience and plastic; silver and silver-plated decorative articles, metallic lighting fixtures; office requisites and artificial flowers; haberdashery; kitchen and pocket knives; hurricane lamps; plush and metal toys, dolls and sport articles; accessories for footwear and leatherwear; alarm and wall clocks; gardening implements; lighting glassware; window glass, mirrors, technical and laboratory glassware.

Imports: — Technological installations and equipment for the light industry sectors (ready-mades, knit-wear, weaving mills, spinning mills, leatherwear, glassware, chinaware, faience etc.); accessories for the equipment of the light industry sectors; licenses, patents, studies, designs, engineering, know-how, technical assistance for the light industry sectors.

ROMTRANS

Bucharest — Romania
196, Calea Rahovei
Telephone: 23 89 20; Telex: 11346; POB: 1311

Secures the best conditions for the forwarding of foreign trade goods from and to all important places in Europe, the Near and Middle East; transit of foreign goods through Romania, for international fairs and exhibitions included, warehousing; transport of collective goods and containers.

TEHNOFORESTEXPORT

Bucharest — Romania
4, Piata Rosetti
Telephone: 16 04 00; 14 30 02; Telex: 11382, 11763, 11362

Exports: — Finished wooden products (furniture, chairs, boats, sports articles, musical instruments, wood containers, windows, doors, prefab cottages); softwood, beech and oak timber, particle and fiberboards — standard and enriched, plywood, panels, veneer, parquetry, pulp timber, charcoal, round beams, paper, pulp, paper and pulp products.

Imports: — Logs, veneer, seagrass, ironmongery and other accessories for furniture; musical instruments and sports articles; specific materials for the wood processing industry (lacquers, dyestuffs, adhesives, paints, polishing paste) which are not included in the import lists of other foreign trade companies; paper pulp, pulp for the footwear industry, paper, cardboard, tegofilm, tegotex, special technical paper (electrical engineering paper and cardboard excluded); special chemicals for the paper and pulp industry which are not included in the import lists of other foreign trade companies.

TEHNOIMPORTEXPORT

Bucharest — Romania
5, Doamnei Street
Telephone: 16 45 70; Telex: 11254; POB: 110

Exports: — Apparatus and installations manufactured by the Nuclear Physics Institute; apparatus (single piece series) produced by the research and design institutes; laboratory and metrology equipment, medical apparatus, atomic physics apparatus; oxyacetylene welding equipment; airplanes, helicopters, gliders, aviation equipment and materials, spare parts; bicycles, motorcycles, components and spare parts; assembling parts and elements, ball bearings, and rollers, bushings; microscopes, teaching aid apparatus and materials; film production equipment and materials; films and recorded tapes not designed for cinematography, TV and radio.

Imports: — Laboratory equipment, medical apparatus and equipment, atomic physics apparatus; airplanes, helicopters, gliders, aviation equipment, bicycles, motorcycles, components and spare parts; pressure-measuring apparatus and instruments; geophysical apparatus; ball bearings and rollers; optical, technical and laboratory glass; fault detectors and gas analysis devices; cameras and materials for film production, radio and TV; duplication equipment; technical clocks; medical and industrial Roentgen apparatus (accessories and components used in the manufacture of Roentgen apparatus included); industrial and laboratory apparatus and equipment used in physical-mechanical tests; optical-mechanical and photogrammetrical apparatus; laboratory furnaces; laboratory pumps; printing materials and equipment; records and recording tapes; films and recorded tapes not designed for cinematography and radio-TV; all types of measurement and gauging apparatus (non-unified system apparatus included); apparatus for measurement of methane gas concentration in mines, spectral analysis apparatus and apparatus for determination of hydrogen, nitrogen, oxygen, and other elements in steel excluded; products, equipment, apparatus and materials for scientific research units including hiring of aforesaid; manufacture lines, assembling parts and elements; cooperation ventures in the field of aeronautics and imports of equipment for aforesaid (if not included in the operations of other specialist foreign trade companies); airport equipment and air navigation protection and control installations; noxious gas and dust protection equipment, diving equipment; machines and equipment for production of lenses, vibration recording and compensating machines and apparatus.

TERRA

Bucharest — Romania
16, Republicii Blvd.
Telephone: 15 30 43; 15 84 83; Telex: 11571, 11341 Terra
Cables: — TERRA BUCHAREST 4; POB: 86

Imports and exports of any kind of commodities, commercial and financial compensation operations, switch, foreign trade operations; carrying out of orders placed by public organizations; joint companies, conclusion of contracts with physical persons, services provided with payment in foreign currency; sale of customs clearance tickets.

UNIVERSAL TRACTOR

Bucharest — Romania
19, Lipscani St.
Telephone: 15 86 20; Telex: 11889; POB: 454 Cables: UNIVERSAL TRACTOR-Bucharest

Subsidiary in Brasov:
5, Turnului St.
Telephone: 10422; Telex: 12335

Exports: — Tire-mounted farming tractors, 35 HP class: U-350; 45 HP class; U-445, V-445, L-445, 445 HCP, 445 HCV, 445 DT, 445 DTE; 55 HP class: U-550 Super, V-550 Super, L-550 Super, 550 DT Super, 550 DTE Super; 65 HP class: U-650 M, 651 M, U-650 Super, 650 DT Super; 80 HP class: U-800, 800 DT; 180 HP class: A-1800 A. Tiremounted industrial tractors, 45 HP class: 445 SD, 445 DTSD, TIH-445; 55 HP class; 550 SD Super, 550 DT-SD Super; 360 HP class; A-3600 IF A-3600 L. Caterpillar farming tractors, 45 HP class: S-445, SV-445, SM-445. Caterpillar industrial tractors, 65 HP class: S-651 LS; 150 HP class: S-1500 LS; 180 HP class: S-1800 IF, S-1800 LS.

Farming Machinery and Equipment: — soil tilling machines and equipment; sowing, planting and fertilizer spraying machines, pest control installations; harvesting and threshing machines; vegetable cleaning, screening and drying equipment; animal husbandry equipment.

Trailers: — 4-ton farming trailers; 3-5 ton motor vehicle trailers; 1800 and 3600 l fuel and lubricant trailed tankers; 4000 l fluid chemical fertilizer trailed tankers; high capacity fodder trailers.

Imports: — Wheel and track-type tractors; bulldozers; farming equipment: — soil tilling; sowing and planting; culture maintenance; harvesting; farming machine engines; hothouse equipment; garden and park equipment.

UZINEXPORTIMPORT

Bucharest — Romania
133, Calea Victoriei
Telephone: 50 25 35; Telex: 11214; POB: 2993

Exports: — Plants and complex installations for the production of equipment and installations in the field of mechanical engineering, electrical engineering and electronics, licenses, invention patents and manufacturing technologies, the relevant CKD; ships, boats, naval equiment, ship repair; thermoelectric power plants, thermal power stations, district heating plants, hydroelectric power plants, hydro-mechanical equipment, diesel electric stations, spare parts; metallurgical and iron and steel installations, the related individual equipment and the outfits, relevant spare parts; food industry installations: refrigerating warehouses, ice factories, milling installations, silos, meat, milk and fruit preparing lines, bread manufacturing factories, the relevant spare parts; cement lines, various individual equipment and outfits, spare parts; studies, designs, know-how, engineering, production lines, technologies for the above-mentioned factories, erection, technical assistance, training.

Imports: — Plants and complete installations for the mechanical engineering industry; equipment for boilers and turbines; equipment for metal surfce protection; complex installations for the food industry, for the scientific institutes and the local industry units; ships, boats, naval equipment and outfits, completion outfits for naval industry included: parts of installations and equipment for cement factories; designs, licenses, technical assistance, training for the imported installations.

VINEXPORT

Bucharest — Romania
41, Brezoianu St.
Telephone: 14 31 94; Telex: 11132; POB: 34

Exports: — Natural bottled and bulk wines; wine brandy; vemouth, sparkling wines; fruit brandies; wine distillates, liqueurs; beer; starch, glucose; concentratedmust; grapes.

VITROCIM

Bucharest — Romania
18, Blanari St.
Telephone: 13 16 38; Telex: 11330 vicim r

Exports: — Binders: — BSS 12/58 Portland cement, anti-sulphatic cements, white cement, building plaster, hydrated plaster, burnt limestone; asbestos dement: — asbestos cement corrugated boards, asbestos cement tubes; hydroinsulating materials: bituminized cardboard, bituminized felting, bituminized cloth; mineral wadding thermal and sound insulating materials: cushions, boards, felts, shells, cord, dialit bricks; marble and marble products: blocks, plates, marmoroc, marble granules, mosaic slabs; ceramic materials: glazed ceramic slas, glazed and nonglared sandstone slabs, faience tiles, ceramic sandstone tubes, tiles, bricks, granulite; wallpapers: PVC wallpaper on paper support; floorings: PVC flooring on textile support; Polirom type thermal and sound-insulating carpet, synthetic moquette; sanitary and heating installation materials: both tubs, radiators, brass sanitary fixtures, cast iron draining pipes, porcelain and enamelled cast iron sanitary articles.

Imports: — Asbestos and asbestos products: — threads, yarns, boards, fabrics, belts, asbestos protection materials, gaskets, cord; cork and cork products: — boards, waste, rounds, granules, gaskets, corks; dyes: — for the ceramic industry.

Chapter 8

VISITING ROMANIA

SIGHTSEEING

Although correspondence can go far towards introducing products and technology and perhaps soliciting inquiries, it is not a very effective sales method in Romania. Initial correspondence and catalogues should be followed up by direct visits. These visits, however, must be organized in advance for maximum effectiveness. An unplanned two or three day visit could be wasted waiting in a hotel lobby.

Including a day or two for sightseeing could be worthwhile, especially if a visitor is accompanied by his or her spouse.

Romania's many tourist attractions include fine natural settings, historical sites and folklore, and attract on an average 7 million visitors a year, mostly from other Eastern European countries. Prices are reasonable.

The Romanian Black Sea Coast is frequented by millions, as are the Romanian spas. The Transylvanian Alps and Carpathians offer some of the best skiing in Europe at very reasonable prices, and the Danube Delta is the refuge for thousands of animals and hundreds of endangered species. Most of the Delta is currently a nature reserve and is open to the public.

Major Romanian tourist areas include the following:

Bucharest—The capital city is a major tourist center with many opportunities for sightseeing and entertainment. Bucharest is surrounded by parks and lakes and is the first stop for most foreign tourists entering the country.

Mountain Resorts—The most popular mountain resorts are located along the Prahova and Timis Valleys cutting through the Carpathians. In recent years, numerous resorts have been built in the areas around Brasov, emphasizing both summer and winter sports and including a major European equestrian center. This region is also known as Dracula country and tourists can visit the haunts of both the historical and fictional characters. Romania has not, however, adequately developed the ghoul market.

The Black Sea Coast—The country's principal summer tourist zone. Sun and water sports are the principal attractions. The City of Constanta, an important economic center and the largest harbor on the Black Sea, stands on the ancient site of the former Greek colony of Tomi, founded in the 7th Century B.C., and has numerous archeological sites. A chain of resorts stretches about 70 miles along the coast from north to south (Mamaia, Constanta, Eforie Nord, Eforie Sud, Costinesti, Neptun, Jupiter, Cap Aurora, Venus, Saturn, and Mangalia) with good hotels and villas and including ancillary combinations for tourists: bowling alleys, miniature golf courses and rental boats. Several of the facilities in this region are known for their spas for the treatment of rheumatism.

The Danube Delta—The largest in Europe, has a unique landscape and a rich variety of wildlife, including large colonies of pelicans and world-class fishing opportunities.

Northern Moldavia—In the northeastern part of Romania, is famous for its ancient traditions and native architecture. The City of Suceava, the former capital of Moldavia in the 14th-16th centuries, preserves many historic and architectural monuments, including the Fortress of Suceava and Scheia.

Central Moldavia—Covers the area around the city of Piatraneamt crossed by the Bistrita and Bicaz Rivers. Major tourist attractions include the Bicaz Gorges, Lacul Rosu (Red Lake), and the historic lake of Bicaz with water sport centers, hotels, and camping sites.

Northern Olentia—Well-known for spas and health resorts such as Govora, Calimanesti, Olanesti, Caciulata and Ocnele Mari.

Neptune Spa, Black Sea

Brahov Resort

USEFUL TIPS

Business Hours

The normal hours for business for foreign trade companies and other government offices are from 7:00 a.m. to 4:00 p.m., Monday through Friday, and from 7:00 a.m. to 12:30 p.m. on Saturday. In Bucharest some office hours are scheduled half an hour later. Most staff members take a short lunch break around 11:30 a.m. or noon. Department stores are open from 8:00 a.m. to 7:00 p.m. Food stores are generally open from 6:00 a.m. to 9:00 p.m.

Official Holidays

Commercial and government holidays are observed January 1 (New Years), May 1 (International Workers Day), and August 23 (National Liberation Day). The day following each of these holidays is also a public holiday.

Clothing

Bucharest has a temperate climate. Like other East European capitals, Bucharest is not well-known for *haute couture.* Further, most Romanians — even businessmen — dress rather casually. In summer one can go to Bucharest's best restaurants in the evenings and be able to count the ties on one hand. In the upper levels of the government and bureaucracy, the directors tend to be slightly more formal (they generally wear a jacket and slacks). Significantly, women tend to pay more attention to their appearance than do men. The vast majority of working women wear smart, if not stylish, dresses while their male counterparts may come to work in jeans and a teeshirt.

Language

Romanians rarely expect foreign businessmen to speak their language. Negotiations may generally be conducted in English. Romanians will generally supply their own interpreters, if necessary. Interpreters can also be secured through the National Travel Office (ONT in Bucharest).

Tipping

Although tips are officially discouraged, they are still appreciated. Romania is, however, a tipper's delight. Tips are only expected for extraordinary service. Even then, 10 percent is generally adequate. For meals, however, a 12 percent gratuity may already be included in the bill and an additional tip is not necessary.

Lighting

Due to the high cost of electricity, Romanian offices, factories and homes are gloomy by Western standards. Energy conservation has gone on for a long time in Romania. It is impolite to comment upon this, as it is a matter of longstanding custom, as well as financial necessity.

Black Market

There is a black market in Romania not only for foreign currencies but for all Western goods. Due to extremely strict enforcement and the inability of most Romanians to dispose of their hard currency (Romanians are by law barred from hard currency stores), the black market offers no real economic opportunity and should be strenuously avoided.

Punctuality

Unlike many other Latin countries, Romanians in the business and government sectors tend to be rather punctual. It is considered bad form to be late for business appointments.

Business Cards

Romanians are fastidious about business cards. After introducing themselves, they will almost invariably hand you one of their cards. The visitor should be prepared to reciprocate.

Shopping

All the major deluxe hotels in Romania, as well as a dozen more locations scattered about Bucharest, have so-called "convertible currency stores". These stores stock goods not generally available to Romanians such as liquor, cigarettes, jewelry and portable tape decks. Since Romanians are prohibited by law from possessing Western currency, these stores are effectively limited to foreign tourists.

Health

Although no innoculations are required for travelers coming from the United States or Europe, it is advisable to be immunized against polio and hepatitis for travel outside urban areas. *Health requirements change. Travelers should check most recent information.*

Time Zone

Romania is in the East European time zone (GMT plus 2 hours); daylight savings time (GMT plus 3 hours) applies from the first Sunday in April to the last Sunday in September.

Electricity

Electricity in Romania is 220 volt, 50 cycle. Romania uses European (continental) style plugs.

Weights/Measures

The metric system is used exclusively in Romania, having been adopted in 1866.

Credit Cards

The following credit cards are valid in Romania: Diner's Club, American Express, Master Card, Access Card, Carte Blanche, Eurocard, Visa and Interbank. Before assuming these cards are accepted in a given establishment, however, visitors are advised to observe signs posted at the establishment or inquire before ordering.

Pharmaceuticals

While Romanian drug stores (chemist's shops) carry a wide range of pharmaceuticals, sometimes even the *generic* names of prescription drugs vary from their U.S. designations. Travelers should ordinarily bring with them sufficient prescription drugs for their stay. In an emergency, however, prescription drugs may be obtained from Chemists #5, 18 Magheru Blvd., telephone: 14 61 16, 24 hours a day.

News

Unlike most communist countries, Romania does not prohibit the ownership of shortwave *radios.* In addition to the local Romanian stations, foreign businessmen may also listen to broadcasts of Voice of America and Radio Free Europe. Romanian *television* is currently broadcast in black and white and color. There are dozens of *newspapers* in Romania, several in English. Romanian news is available in most hotels in several foreign languages. Foreign newspapers and periodicals are not generally available in Romania.

Weekends

For the business traveler, ONT-CARPATI, National Tourist Office, offers a number of 2 and 3-day tours of the Bucharest area and outlying regions. These range from excursions to the Carpathians to 2 days on the Black Sea coast. There are also specialized tours emphasizing the wine country, monasteries, folklore, history and castles. In addition, ONT-CARPATI can arrange "customized" tours with drivers and interpreters. Hotels can also advise business travelers of events in Bucharest over weekends. These include sporting events, motion pictures, opera and symphony. Romanians play hard on the day and a half allocated to recreation (Saturday noon to Sunday evening). The parks and lakes around Bucharest are jammed with people during this period and numerous cultural events are scheduled at this time.

Telephone/Telex

Telephone and telex facilities are available at most major hotels. As in other European countries, telephone/telex facilities are also available at post offices.

As is the case with most European countries, however, it is almost always cheaper to receive telephone/telex messages than to send them. Many businessmen arrange to have their offices call them at predetermined times, rather than initiating calls themselves.

Foreign companies which establish offices in Romania obtain telephones and telexes by contacting ARGUS. The bills for telex and telephone are, however, settled at the CARPATI National Tourist Office.

Housing

Housing for foreign nationals temporarily (or permanently) resident in Romania can be obtained through the CARPATI National Travel Office. Rental of apartments ranges from $7 to $70 per day depending upon location and size. ARGUS receives a modest commission for arranging housing accommodations.

Tourist Information

The "Carpati-Bucharesti" National Tourist Office offers the following services: reservations of rooms at hotels, motels, camping sites, *etc;* currency exchange; sightseeing tours of Bucharest; bookings for tickets for performances and sporting events; reservations in spas; rent-a-car; booking of train tickets; multilingual guides; and transfers to airports and railway stations. These services can also be arranged through most major hotels. *Carpati-Bucharesti National Tourist Office, 7 Magheru Blvd. Telephone: 145160, TELEX: 11270 CarpatR.*

CUSTOMS REGULATIONS

Foreign citizens entering Romania are entitled to bring with them the following products duty free: liquor (2 liters), cigarettes (200) or tobacco (300 grams), cigars (300 grams). Any quantity in excess of these amounts is subject to customs duties as follows: cigars, 40 percent; liquor, 50 percent.

Samples

Samples and models without commercial value (cut, punched and stapled on cards) may be imported duty-free. Samples of commercial value may be temporarily imported on the basis of ATA carnets. Should these commercial value samples remain in Romania, they must be assigned to a Romanian foreign trade company. Such samples may also be assigned duty free to educational establishments, research centers or medical institutions.

Businessmen bring into Romania medicines for personal use proportionate to the duration of their stay. Medicine, clothes, food, cigarettes, up to 4000 lei per year for each person of age and 2000 lei for each child are exempt from customs duties for the permanent staff of foreign offices in Romania.

Literature

Visitors should be aware that customs authorities may confiscate certain types of prohibited literature. Included in this category are seditious material, political propaganda and pornography. It is also not allowed to import books and other literature for resale (even in small quantities) without appropriate clearances from the authorities.

AIR TRAVEL

TAROM (Transporturi Aeriene Romoine) and LAR (Liniile Aeriene Romaine) provide local services from 16 airports. These Romanian companies also operate 36 overseas routes.

Three international airports (Bucharest, Constanta and Timisoara) provide flight services.

Airlines

AEROFLOT
35, N. Balcescu Blvd.
Bucharest
Telephone: 16 74 31

AIR FRANCE
35, N. Balcescu Blvd.
Bucharest
Telephone: 13 95 52

ALITALIA
41, Magheru Blvd.
Bucharest
Telephone: 59 75 20

AUA
7, N. Balcescu Blvd.
Bucharest
Telephone: 14 12 21

BRITISH AIRWAYS
22, N. Balcescu Blvd.
Bucharest
Telephone: 16 30 22

CSA
3-5, Batistei St.
Bucharest
Telephone: 14 80 59 and
16 47 05
Otopeni Airport
Telephone: 33 31 37

INTERFLUG
31, Soseaua Kiseleff
Bucharest
Telephone: 33 23 62
TELEX: 11-565
Otopeni Airport
Telephone: 33 31 37/521

LOT
41, Magheru Blvd.
Bucharest
Telephone: 59 25 75

LUFTHANSA
18, Magheru Blvd.
Bucharest
Telephone: 12 99 50

MALEV
Otopeni International Airport
Telephone: 33 31 37/526

PANAM
4, N. Balcescu Blvd.
Bucharest
Telephone: 13 63 61

SABENA
24, N. Balcescu Blvd.
Bucharest
Telephone: 15 12 26

SWISSAIR
18, Magheru Blvd.
Bucharest
Telephone: 13 66 76

CAR, BUS AND RAIL

Cars may be rented either with or without a driver at all major hotels. Rental, with driver, (minimum 4 hours) is $18 per hour; without a driver, $27 per day plus 25¢ per kilometer.

Taxis

Taxis in Bucharest may be ordered through the hotel doorman or by dialing 053. Unless you speak Romanian, however, it is better to have someone call for you as the taxi switchboard operators have a great deal of difficulty understanding English messages. All taxis are metered and are very reasonable.

Gypsy

In addition, it sometimes seems that every tenth Romanian with an automobile is prepared to take you anywhere you want to go at about double the rate of the official taxicabs. This is a booming business due to the relative scarcity of cabs in the city.

Foreign businessmen are advised *not* to use the facilities of the "gypsy" cab system. Not only is it highly illegal (passengers may be subject to arrest as well as the drivers), they are expensive, the drivers don't know Bucharest as well as official chauffeurs and there can be significant insurance problems in the event of an accident.

Public Transport

Bucharest has many inexpensive, but often crowded buses and streetcars. A new subway system was inaugurated in 1979 and is currently undergoing expansion.

Driving to Bucharest from December through February is not advised, as mountain passes can be hazardous. Otherwise, the main roads are reasonably good.

Rail

Rail facilities are available for domestic and international travel. The daily Wiener-Walzer Express from Vienna takes roughly 20 hours to reach Bucharest.

Purchase

A foreigner stationed in Romania may opt to buy a Romanian DACIA 1300 automobile for local use through the COMTURIST Agency (approximate price: $5,000).

HOTELS

Foreigners are usually expected to settle their hotel accounts in hard currency. All deluxe category hotels, however, accept major credit cards. At the hard currency rate, Romanian hotels in the deluxe category are reasonably priced compared to similar accommodations elsewhere in Europe.

The following are the *deluxe* category hotels in *Bucharest*:

Ambassador
10, Gh. Magheru Blvd.
Telephone: 11 04 40

Athenee Palace
1-3, Episcopiei Street
Telephone: 14 08 99
TELEX: 162

Bucharesti
65-69 Calea Victoriei
Telephone: 15 46 40

Bulevard
1, Gh. Gheorghiu-Dej Blvd.
Telephone: 13 13 08

Continental
56, Calea Victoriei
Telephone: 14 53 49
TELEX: 10380

Dorobanti
1-3, Calea Dorobanti
Telephone: 11 08 60

Flora
1, Poligrafiei Blvd.
Telephone: 18 46 40

Intercontinental
4-6, N. Balcescu Blvd.
Telephone: 14 04 00
TELEX: 54 15 42

Lido
5, Gh. Magheru Blvd.
Telephone: 14 49 30
TELEX: 161

National
Republicii Blvd.
Telephone: 13 01 99

Nord
143, Calea Grivitei
Telephone: 50 60 81

The following are *first class* category hotels in *Bucharest:*

Minerva
2, Lt. Lemnea Street
Telephone: 50 60 10

Modern
46, Republicii Blvd.
Telephone: 16 43 20

Parc
3, Poligrafiei Blvd.
Telephone: 18 09 50

Union
11, 13 Decembrie Street
Telephone: 13 26 40

Hotel reservations may be guaranteed in the following manner:

- By reservations made by a partner travel agency of the National Travel Office (ONT);

- By reservations by Telex and letters with the National Travel Office (ONT) including 50 percent of the sum in advance; the National Travel Office is entitled to make reservations for hotels throughout the country;

- By the Intercontinental Hotel chain for guaranteed reservations at "Intercontinental" and "Continental" hotels in Bucharest.

RESTAURANTS

Romania has thousands of bars, brasseries, and beer gardens. There is a local custom, however, dating back many years which dictates that only spirits are sold in bars while beer and wine are sold in brasseries. Except for the Black Sea coastal resorts where beer is sold in bars, you must order your lighter alcoholic beverages in brasseries, restaurants or beer gardens.

As in most Eastern European countries, imported hard liquor sold in bars can be very expensive and one is generally better off buying a bottle for the room or sticking to the local offerings which, in the case of beer and wine, are exceptionally good.

Brasseries

Ambasador
10, Magheru Blvd.
Telephone: 11 63 87

Berlin
4, C. Mille Street
Telephone: 14 46 52

Bulevard
1, Gh. Gheorghiu-Dej Blvd.
Telephone: 13 13 08

Cismigiu
22, Gh. Gheorghiu-Dej Blvd.
Telephone: 15 61 70

Dorobanti
1-3, Calea Doro-banti
Telephone: 11 08 60

Flora
1, Poligrafiei Blvd.
Telephone: 18 36 83

Athenee Palace
1-3, Episcopiei Street
Telephone: 14 08 99

Bucuresti
34, Calea Victoriei
Telephone: 13 44 82

Cina
1, C.A. Rosetti Street
Telephone: 14 02 17

Continental
56, Calea Victoriei
Telephone: 14 53 49

Dunarea
(brasserie, wine-cellar, summer terrace, confectioner's)
3, N. Balcescu Blvd.
block of flats, "Dunarea"
Telephone: 16 27 26

Gradinita
(brasserie and summer terrace)
24 A, Magheru Blvd.
Telephone: 59 54 30

Inter-Continental
(Madrigal, Balada, Corso, Self-Service)
4-6, N. Balcescu Blvd.
Telephone: 14 04 00

Lido
5, Magheru Blvd.
Telephone: 14 49 30

Marul de Aur
163, Calea Victoriei
Telephone: 50 76 48

Miorita
24, Soseaua Kiseleff
(Herastrau Park)
Telephone: 17 10 95

Modern
46, Republicii Blvd.
Telephone: 16 43 20

Monte Carlo
Cismigiu Gardens
Telephone: 13 13 44

Nan Jing
(within the "Minerva" hotel – Chinese cuisine)
2, Lt. D. Lemnea Street
Telephone: 50 60 10

Nord
143, Calea Grivitei
Telephone: 50 60 81

Parc
3, Polifgrafei Blvd.
Telephone: 18 16 49

Parcul Trandafirilor
9, Piata Cosmonautilor
Telephone: 12 17 43

Pescarus
Herastrau Park
Telephone: 79 46 52

Tei
5, Doamna Ghica Tei Street
Telephone: 87 54 30

The Spanish Salon
116, Calea Victoriei
Telephone: 59 53 45

Turn
25, 13 Decembrie Street
Telephone: 13 69 50

Restaurants with Romanian Cuisine

Carul cu Bere (Beer House)
3, Stavropoleos Street
Telephone: 16 37 93

Crama Domneasca
(Princely Wine-Cellar)
13, Selari Street
Telephone: 14 28 68

Doina
4, Soseaua Kiseleff
Telephone: 16 30 95

Ducur
2, Poenaru Bordea Street
Telephone: 123 60 54

Hanul Manuc (Manuc Inn)
62, 30 Decembreie Street
Telephone: 13 14 15

La doi cocosi (At Two Roosters)
6, Soseaua Straulesti
Telephone: 67 19 98

Parcul Privighetorilor
Padurea Baneasa
(Baneasa Forest)
Telephone: 33 05 01

Rapsodia
2, Selari Street
Telephone: 15 54 13

Night Life

While Bucharest may not be Paris in terms of night life, there are still a few interesting places to visit after dark. Nightclubs include:

Athenee Palace
1-3 Episcopiei Street
Telephone: 14 09 88

Doina
4 Soseaua Kiseleff
Telephone: 16 30 95

Melody
2 Pictor Verona Street
Telephone: 12 92 00

USEFUL DIPLOMATIC ADDRESSES

Official information and assistance regarding trade with Romania can be obtained from economic and trade counselors at the following Romanian missions abroad:

Romanian Embassies and Trade Offices

ALBANIA
Embassy
2 Temistoki Germenji
Tirana
Tel: 2041
Cables: ROMANOCOM

ALGERIA
Embassy
24 Arezki Hydra
El Mouradia
Algiers
TELEX: 52915

ANGOLA
Embassy
66 Rua 5 de Outubro
Malanga
Luanda
Tel: 34918; 36757
TELEX: 3022 Abron An.

UNITED ARAB EMIRATES
Trade Representative
Almaktoum St.
Omar Bin Abdulla Building
Flat No. 12
Deira-Dubai
Tel: 432361; 432408
TELEX: 45880
Cables: ROMANOCOM

ARGENTINA
Embassy
962, Avenida Arroyo
Buenos Aires
Tel: 392-2630
TELEX: 1745

AUSTRALIA
General Consulate
33, Old South Head Road
NSWI 2026
Bondi
Sydney
Tel: 305714; 305718
TELEX: 22312

AUSTRIA
Trade Representative
25, Therresianumgasse
Vienna IV
Tel: 65 16 20; 65 44 33
TELEX: 132169 AMROM A

BANGLADESH
Trade Representative
Road 74 House —
33 Gulshan Model Town
Dacca
Tel: 30 01 28; 30 14 67
TELEX: 65739 ROMC BJ

BELGIUM
Embassy
105, Rue Gabrielle
1180 Brussels
Tel: 345 00 40; 345 26 80
TELEX: 2/21859
Cables: ROMANOCOM

BENIN
Embassy
POB: 359
Cotonou
Tel: 30 09 73

BOLIVIA
Embassy
Calle Capitan Ravelo (pasaje
Isaac G. Eduarde) no. 2123
Casilla: 20879
La Paz
Tel: 37 86 32
TELEX: 3260

BRAZIL
Embassy
Avenida das Nacoes
Sector Norte, Lote 6
Brasilia
Tel: 2 26 07 46
TELEX: 061-1283

Commercial Office
526, Rua Cosme Velho
Rio de Janeiro
Tel: 225 22 12; 225 00 60
TELEX: 02121635

Commercial Office
Av. Brigadeiro Faria Lima
Nr. 1390; floor 6, Conjunto 61
CEP 01452
Sao Paolo
Tel: (011) 2107109
TELEX: (011) 227331 ROM. BR.

BULGARIA
Embassy
10, Dimiter Polianov St.
POB: 263
Sofia
Tel: 44 26 15; 44 11 10;
44 32 02
TELEX: 22554
Cables: ROMANOCOM

BURMA
Embassy
71, Mission Road
Rangoon
TELEX: 21 323

BURUNDI
Embassy
Rue Pierre Ngendandumwe
POB: 2770
Bujumbura
Tel: 4135

CAMEROON
Commercial Office
Rue 27 Aout 1940
Immeuble Societe Civile
Immobiliere Africaine, 2e etage
POB: 6212
Yaounde
Tel: 23 39 86
TELEX: 8417 AMBARSR

CANADA
General Consulate
3664, Mountain Street
POB: H3 G-2 A8
Montreal
Tel: 842-1779; 842-1770
TELEX: 05268571
Cables: ROMANOCOM

CENTRAL AFRICAN REPUBLIC
Embassy
POB: 907
Bangui
Tel: 2766
TELEX: 5223

CHILE
Embassy
2955 Calle Benjamin —
Portado Vitacure
Santiago
Tel: 48 25 29
TELEX: 44 03 78 IPT
Booth Santiago Chile
Cables: ROMANOCOM Beijing

PEOPLE'S REPUBLIC OF CHINA
Embassy
Ri-Tan-Lu-Dong-Er-Jie
Beijing
Tel: 52 34 42; 52 33 72
TELEX: 41238

COLOMBIA
Embassy
Carrera 7 a No. 92—58
Apartado Aereo: 25408
Bogota
Tel: 256 64 58; 256 63 98
TELEX: 441238
Cables: ROMANOCOM

CONGO
Embassy
POB: 26
Brazzaville
Tel: 81 24 99
TELEX: 5259 KG

COSTA RICA
Embassy
POB: 10321
San Jose
Tel: 310741
TELEX: 2337 Embarom

CUBA
Embassy
Calle Hel Vedado
Havana
Tel: 32 43 03; 32 16 71

CZECHOSLOVAKIA
Embassy
5, Nerudova St.
Prague 1
Tel: 53 81 81; 53 87 37
TELEX: 121506 arom
Cables: ROMACECO

General Consulate
11, Frana Krala
Bratislava
TELEX: 92307

CYPRUS
Embassy
37, Tompazis St. (Likavitos)
POB: 2210
Nicosia
Tel: 43785
TELEX: 2431 ROMCOM CY
Cables: ROMANOCOM

DENMARK
Embassy
27, Strandagervej,
2900 Hellerup
Copenhagen
Tel: 62 29 62
TELEX: 27017
Cables: ROMCOM D.K.

ECUADOR
Embassy
Calle Antonio Flores Dijon
no. 261
Quito
Tel: 450590
TELEX: 2230 EMBARO ED
Cables: ROMANOCOM

EGYPT
Embassy
6, Kamel Mohamed St.; Zamalek
Cairo
Tel: 69 81 07; 80 53 26
TELEX: 93807

Commercial Office
2, Gomhoria
Hamza Building, 1st floor, flat 10
Port Said
Tel: 4384
Cables: ROMANOCOM

Commercial Office
4, Pharaoh St.
Alexandria
Tel: 30 656
Cables: ROMANOCOM

ETHIOPIA
Embassy
POB: 62
Addis-Ababa
Cables: ROMANOCOM
TELEX: 21168

FINLAND
Embassy
24, Stenbackinkatu, Hiki 25
Helsinki
Tel: 41 36 24; 41 44 14
TELEX: 121041, roamb sf
Cables: ROMANOCOM

FRANCE
Embassy
5, Rue de l'Exposition —
Paris VII-e
Tel: 705 57 64
TELEX: 270793
Cables: ROMANOCOM

GABON
Embassy
POB: 3892
Libreville
Tel: 73 27 87
TELEX: 5359

GERMAN DEMOCRATIC REPUBLIC
Embassy
23 Parkstrasse 110 Berlin;
Pankow
Berlin
Tel: 482 55 94; 480 01 76
TELEX: 112305
Cables: ROMANOCOM

FEDERAL REPUBLIC OF GERMANY
Embassy
5300 Bonn-1
Legions Weg 14
Tel: 0228 67 00 01-5
TELEX: 8869792

General Consulate
79, Mathernhornstrasse
1, Berlin West 38
Tel: 030/803 30 18
TELEX: 185473

GHANA
Embassy
11, Watson Avenue House
POB: 3735
Accra
Tel: 74 655
TELEX: 2027

GREECE
Embassy
7, Emanuel Benaki St.,
Paleo Psihico
Athens
Tel: 6716006; 6718020
TELEX: 215301 — ROMC GR

GUINEA
Embassy
9, Boulevard de la Presidence
POB: 847
Conakry
Tel: 3478

HUNGARY
Embassy
XII Thokoly nt. 72
Budapest
Tel: 227-689; 425-552; 425-773
TELEX: 225847
Cables: ROMANOCOM

INDIA
Embassy
52 A VASANT MARG VASANT VIHAR
New Delhi
Tel: 664447/670700/676111
TELEX: 031-2287
Cables: ROMANOCOM

Trade Representative
Apeejay House
Dinshaw Wacha Road
Churchgate Reclamation
Bombay 400020
Tel: 22 00 74
TELEX: 011-4023
Cables: ROMANOCOM

Trade Representative
27, Khader Nawaz Khan Road
Madras 600006
Tel: 8 36 24; 8 83 87
TELEX: 041-542 ROMS IN
Cables: ROMANOCOM

INDONESIA
Embassy
42 A, J.L. Teuku Cik Ditiro
Jakarta
Tel: 35 48 47; 34 95 24
TELEX: 45008
Cables: ROMANOCOM

IRAN
Embassy
12, Fakhrabad Ave.
Teheran 5
Tel: 75 99 11; 75 99 22
TELEX: 212791 romc-ir

IRAQ
Embassy
5, Sadoun St. Building Al-Safar
Masbah 203/7/19
Baghdad
Tel: 93048-93040
TELEX: 2268
Cables: ROMANOCOM

ISRAEL
Embassy
24, Adam Hacoen
Tel-Aviv
Tel: 24 24 82; 24 73 79
TELEX: 33867

ITALY
Embassy
36, Via Nicolo Tartaglia
Rome
Tel: 87 25 41
TELEX: 610249
Cables: ROAMB

Commercial Bureau
3, Via Orti
Milan 20122
Tel: 58 12 87; 58 10 78
TELEX: 310446
Cables: ROMANOCOM

JAPAN
Embassy
Nishi Azabu, 16—19, 3-Chome-
Minato-Ku, 106
Tokyo
Tel: 479 0411; 479 0311
TELEX: 22664
Cables: ROMANOCOM

JORDAN
Embassy
Shmeishani
POB: 2406
Amman
Tel: 66 31 61
Cables: ROMANOCOM
TELEX: 21860

KENYA
Embassy
Norfolk Towers St., flat 42 A
POB: 48412
Nairobi
Tel: 27 515
Cables: ROMANOCOM

KOREA (NORTH)
Embassy
Din Sen Don 1
Pyong-Yang
Tel: 246; 204; 253
TELEX: ROMCOM — Py 481

KUWAIT
Embassy
Jabria District; zone 3; Building
53; ap. 14—15; fifth floor
POB: 11149
Kuwait
TELEX: 22148
Cables: ROMANOCOM

LEBANON
Embassy
Secteur 36 Manara,
77, Rue Raouche
Beirut, Imm. Khaled
POB: 8184
Abdo.
TELEX: 20661
Cables: ROMANOCOM

LIBERIA
Embassy
81, Sekou Toure Av.
POB: 1042
Monrovia
Tel: 21173
TELEX: 4202
Cables: ROMANOCOM

LIBYA
Embassy
POB: 4747
Tripoli
Tel: 4 40 27
TELEX: 20482
Cables: ROMANOCOM

MALAYSIA
Embassy
114, Jalan Damai
Kuala Lumpur
Tel: 48 20 65
TELEX: 30362
Cables: ROMANOCOM
KUALALUMPUR

MEXICO
Embassy
311, Sofocles St.
Colonia Polanco Chapultepec
Mexico City
Tel: 545 53 77
TELEX: AMROMME 017 75-868
Cables: ROMANOCOM MEXIC

MONGOLIA
Embassy
18 Miradom St.
Ulan Bator
Tel: 2 16 12
TELEX: ROMANOTORG ULAN
BATOR U-BT 252
Cables: ROMANOTORG

MOROCCO
Embassy
10, Rue Ouezzane
Rabat
Tel: 34486
TELEX: 31079

Economic Section
19, Rue Bournazel
Casablanca
Tel: 27 16 50
TELEX: 22043

MOZAMBIQUE
Embassy
59, Rua Antonio Caldeira
POB: 4647
Maputo
TELEX: 6-397 mo

NETHERLANDS
Embassy
37—39, Casthevel
The Hague
Tel: (070) 54 15 80; 54 15 87
TELEX: 32189
Cables: ROMANOCOM

NIGERIA
Embassy
30, Reymond Njoku Road,
S.W. Ikoyi
POB: 595
Lagos
Tel: 2730
TELEX: 21374

NORWAY
Embassy
51, Oscarsgate
Oslo
Tel: 43 16 74; 44 15 12
TELEX: 16844
Cables: ROMANOCOM

PAKISTAN
Trade Representative
245/2/H P.E.C.H.S.
Karachi 29
Tel: 4 301 31; 43 01 32
TELEX: 28883 rocom pk

PERU
Embassy
Avenida Orrantia no. 690
San Isidoro
POB: 10049
Lima
Tel: 22 45 67
TELEX: 25624

PHILIPPINES
Embassy
1253 Acacia Road
Dasmarinas Village
Makati
Postal code: 3117
Manila
Tel: 87 67 67
TELEX: 45460 ROMCOM PM

POLAND
Embassy
10, Chopina St.
Warsaw
Tel: 28 33 00
TELEX: 813420
Cables: ROMAG

PORTUGAL
Embassy
5, Rua Sao Caetano
Lisbon
Tel: 66 64 63
TELEX: 13377 Ambrom

SENEGAL
Embassy
Boulevard de l'Est
4 rue Point E
POB: 3171
Dakar
Tel: 22 19 13
TELEX: 3115

SINGAPORE
Embassy
48, Jalan Harom Sotangkai,
Singapore 1025
Tel: 4 68 34 24/5
TELEX: romano rs 22184

SOMALIA
Economic Agency
POB: 651
Mogadishu
Tel: 23 871

SPAIN
Embassy
157, Avenida Alfonso XIII
Madrid 16
Tel: 45 87 75; 47 97 49
TELEX: 22433 rocom e

SRI LANKA
Embassy
71 A, Dharmapala-Mawatha
Colombo 7
Tel: 54 98 19

SUDAN
Embassy
Street 47; Plot 67
POB: 1652
Khartoum
Tel: 4 17 31; 4 42 98
TELEX: 24188

SWEDEN
Embassy
36, Ostermalmsgatan, 11426-S
Stockholm
Tel: 08/10 28 52; 10 28 56;
10 28 72; 10 23 96; 10 23 98
TELEX: 10166 Agerom S
Cables: ROMANOCOM

SWITZERLAND
Embassy
20, Brunnadernstrasse
Berne 3000
Tel: (031) 44 64 54; 44 64 55
TELEX: 32273
Cables: ROMANOCOM

SYRIA
Embassy
Ibrahim Hanano St.
POB: 4322
Damascus
Tel: 71 73 23; 71 00 51;
71 00 52

TANZANIA
Economic Agency
Upaga East Plot 408
POB: 2408
TELEX: 411305 romcom sy
Cables: ROMANOCOM
Dar Es Salaam
Tel: 27057

THAILAND
Embassy
Su kumwit Rd, Soi 10,
Nr. 39 Road
Bangkok
Tel: 252-8515; 251-0280;
251-6421 3021
TELEX: ROMCOM TH 2872
Cables: ROMANOCOM

TUNISIA
Embassy
6, Rue Magon Notre Dame
Tunis
Tel: 28 11 75

TURKEY
Consulate General
55, Siraselviler Cadessi, Tacsim
Istanbul Beyoglu
Tel: 1 44 82 51
TELEX: 24638 ROM
Cables: ROMANOCOM

Embassy
4, Bukres Sokak
Ankara, CANKAYA
Tel: 27 52 30; 27 15 30
TELEX: 42760 rotm-tr
Cables: ROMANOCOM

UNITED STATES OF AMERICA
Trade Promotion Office
350 South Figueroa Street
Suite 447
Los Angeles, California 90071
Tel: (213) 614-1107
TELEX: 067093 ROMTRAD

Commercial Office
573—577 Third Avenue
New York, New York
Tel: (212) 682-9120; 9121; 9122; 9123
TELEX: ROMANOCOM 420326

Embassy
1607 23 St., N.W.
Washington, DC 20008
Washington
Tel: (202) 232-4747
TELEX: 02340-089671

Trade Promotion Office
2255 Lenox Road, N.E.
Suite 1-1
Atlanta, Georgia 30324
Tel: (404) 636-6044
TELEX: Romtrade

Trade Promotion Office
515 Tallowood Rd., Suite 20
Houston, Texas 77024
Tel: (713) 465-7821
TELEX: Romtr 203239

UNITED KINGDOM
Embassy
4, Palace Green
London W 8
London
Tel: (01) 937 9666
TELEX: 22232
Cables: ROMANOCOM

UNION OF THE SOVIET SOCIALIST REPUBLICS
Embassy
64, Mosfilmovskaia St.
Moscow
Tel: 1 43 04 22; 1 43 28 09
TELEX: 7359-7360
Cables: ROMANOTORG

Trade Promotion Office
105 W. Madison St.
Room 1505
Chicago, Illinois 60602
Tel: (312) 782-4463; 4464
TELEX: ROMTRADE

URUGUAY
Embassy
Frederico Abadio 2940
Apto 102
Montevideo
Tel: 70 75 20
TELEX: 23176

VENEZUELA
Embassy
Avda Principal de la Castellana
no. 42
Caracas
Tel: 336324

VIETNAM
Embassy
5, Le Hong Phong St.
Hanoi
Tel: 52014

YEMEN
Embassy
Abyan Beach Road nr.
106 A—B Khormakser
POB: 6049
Aden
Tel: 23522—24366
Cables: ROMANOCOM

YEMEN ARAB REPUBLIC
Economic Agency
POB: 2169
Sanaa
Tel: 24 79 21
TELEX: 2361

YUGOSLAVIA
Embassy
70 Kneza Milosa St.
Belgrade
Tel: 64 61 51; 64 60 71
TELEX: 11441
Cables: ROMANOCOM

ZAIRE
Embassy
POB: 2242
Kinshasa
Tel: 30577; 30 988
TELEX: 21316

ZAMBIA
Embassy
POB: 1224
Lusaka
Tel: 5 21 82
Cables: ROMANOCOM

NEW ZEALAND
Embassy
31 Doris Gordon Crescent,
Crofton Downs
Wellington
Tel: 792951
TELEX: NZ 31259
Cables: ROMANOCOM

ZIMBABWE
Embassy
105, 4th St.
POB: 2140
Harare
Tel: 2 54 55
TELEX: 4797-ZW

BIBLIOGRAPHY

Following are a few useful publications:

Chemistry

The Romanian Journal of Chemistry, available from PUBLICOM. This publication is free of charge and outlines the available products from the Romanian chemical industry and gives some reference to required imports.

Contracts

The Romanian-American Economic Council is an organization of joint cooperation between the U.S. Chamber of Commerce and the Chamber of Commerce and Industry of Romania. The Council publishes a number of technical documents, one of the most useful of which is: *The Rules And Contractual Clauses Utilized In Romanian-American Commercial Relations.* It is available through the U.S. Chamber of Commerce or from the Foreign Trade Publicity Agency, Bucharest, Romania, 22, N. Balcescu Boulevard; Telex: 11347.

Engineering

Romanian Engineering published by PUBLICOM. This is a quarterly issued and edited under the auspices of the Chamber of Commerce and Industry, the Mechanical Engineering Industry Ministry and the Machine Tools, Electrical, and Electrical Industry Ministry. It carries articles on the production and development prospects of Romanian mechanical engineering, export offers and joint venture potentials.

Economic Information

A Romanian manual dealing with commercial relations is the *Economic and Commercial Guide to Romania,* published by PUBLICOM.

Forest Products

Foresta published by PUBLICOM under the auspices of the Chamber of Commerce and Industry and the Forest Economy and Building Materials Ministry. This publication treats the issues of production, research, expiration and cooperation in the area of woodworking, furniture making and building materials. These pamphlets are available from ILEXIM, 3,13 Decembrie Street, Bucharest, Romania.

Foreign Trade

ILEXIM issues a quarterly periodical, *Romanian Foreign Trade.* This periodical lists all new Romanian products available for the export market. It is available from ILEXIM Press, Import-Export Department, Bucharest, 3,13 Decembrie Street; POB 136-137; Telex: 11226, yearly subscription rate U.S. $44.00

History and Politics

Romanian Historical Itinerary, 1944-1974, by Cristian Popisteanu and Petre Panzaru, published by Editura Enciclopedica Romana, Bucharest, 1974. This handbook is as much a political document as an historical one, emphasizing the rationale for Romania's current political, economic and social policies.

The Concise History history series includes pamphlet-sized books on Romanian sociology, education, film, language, law, arts, theatre, geography and philosophy. They are available from Editura Stiinfifica Si Enciclopedica, Bucharest.

Investing

Trading and Investing in Romania, is a 23-page Overseas Business Reports, published by the U.S. Department of Commerce. Available from Superintendent of Documents, U.S. Government Printing Office, Washington, D.C. 20402, OBR78-33 (September, 1978).
Doing Business in Romania 1979, published by PUBLICOM is a short (77 page) pamphlet written from an official point of view.

Romania — Documents, Events, published by Agerpres (Romanian News Agency), Scienteia Square, Bucharest, Telephone: 18 20 30. These short booklets are published almost weekly and include topics of current interest, government pronouncements, reports of RCP meetings, etc.

Joint Ventures

Joint Venture Agreements In Romania, U.S. Department of Commerce, 1977, available from the U.S. Government Printing Office, Stock NO. 003-009-00242-7. Although somewhat dated, this publication provides a detailed analysis of joint venture agreements both under U.S. and Romanian law.

The Socialist Republic of Romania Promotes the Turning to Account of Other States' Natural Resources by Joint Cooperation Ventures, available from Publicom. As the title suggests, this short pamphlet presents heavy reading to foreigners interested in joint ventures.

Machinery

A quarterly review of new developments in Romanian equipment machinery is available from PUBLICOM under the auspices of the Chamber of Commerce and Industry, Bucharest, Romania, 22, N. Balcescu Boulevard; Telephone: 14 75 35, Telex: 11374. This magazine lists newly available products n the aeronautical, automotive, computers, electric power generation, machine tools, machinery, railway and technical areas.

Romania — General

Romania, An Encyclopaedic Survey, is published by Editura Stiintifica Si Enciclopedica, Bucharest, 1980. This manual gives a general overview of Romania in one volume. It is available from Romanian Embassies abroad.

Romania General Survey. This official booklet, also available from the Romanian missions, is more subjective than *Romania, An Encyclopaedic Survey,* and more extensive.

Romania Facts and Figures published by Editura Stiintifica Si Enciclopedica, Bucharest, is a companion book to *Romania, An Encyclopaedic Survey.*

Romania At A Glance, published by PUBLICOM and designed primarily for tourists, with some reference to commercial relations.

Romanian Trade Entities

Your Commercial Partners In Romania, published by PUBLICOM under the auspices of the Chamber of Commerce and Industry, Bucharest, Romania, 22, N. Balcescu Boulevard; Telephone; 14 75 35, Telex: 11374. This is a compendium of all the authorized trading companies in Romania and an analysis of their import and export needs.

Statistics

Romania Economic Data, edited under the sponsorship of the Chamber of Commerce and Industry of Romania by PUBLICOM (The Foreign Trade Publicity Agency), Bucharest, Romania, 22, N. Balescu Boulevard.

Statistical Year Book of the Socialist Republic of Romania, edited by the Statistics Central Board.

Trade Laws

Romanian Foreign Trade Law published by PUBLICOM (the Foreign Trade Publicity Agency) under the auspices of the Chamber of Commerce and Industry. This handbook is available from Romanian Embassies abroad.

The Digest of General Laws of Romania, published by the Legislative Council of Romania, is an authoritative index of all financial/commercial laws of Romania. It is an absolute necessity for any company doing serious business in the country. It is available from the Romanian Embassies.